Becoming Emotionally Intelligent

Notes from my journey

Nidhi Gupta Nihalani

Table Of Contents

Preface iv

Chapter 1: The Quesadilla of Mind 7

Chapter 2: Laying the Foundation, The Two Pillars 11

Chapter 3: Knowledge Vs Knowing, The Hidden Gap 21

Chapter 4: Self-responsibility, Freedom of Acceptance.......28

Chapter 5: Emotions, The Invisible Strings 35

Chapter 6: Anger, Nature's Gift..41

Chapter 7: Fear, Acquired Burden..52

Chapter 8: Joy and Sorrow, Siamese twins...........................60

Chapter 9: Selfishness, Misunderstood Virtue 68

Chapter 10: Obligation, Ultimate Motivator 75

Chapter 11: Values, My Personal Treasure 82

Chapter 12: From Awareness to Control...............................88

Chapter 13: Control Vs Manage, The Vital Shift 92

Chapter 14: Expansion, The Remaining Two Pillers............97

Chapter 15: Empathy, The Invisible Bridge 100

Chapter 16: Listening, The Empathy Tool..........................110

Chapter 17: Communication Style, Keyhole to Motive 117

Chapter 18: Assertiveness, Navigating Hard Talks 128

Chapter 19: Conflicts, Threat or Opportunity?..................133

Chapter 20: I First, The Conclusion 140

Chapter 21: EI, Relevance in the Age of AI 144

Epilogue 148

Becoming Emotionally Intelligent

Notes from my journey

Preface

Something that started with a simple conversation – the kind that slips into your evening without warning. A close friend and I were talking about life, growth, all the usual spirals. And somewhere in the middle of that, she said, *"You should write about Emotional Intelligence."*

I laughed. Not the dismissive kind – the what-would-I-even - say kind.

"I anyway don't like preaching," I told her. *"I'd rather someone learn quietly – by observing who I am, and how I show up."*

She smiled. Said nothing more. But the thought stayed.

This wasn't the first time I'd heard it. During my sessions, many people, perhaps drawn to something in the way I navigate things, had offered similar feedback.

And then, one day, it clicked.

Maybe that is the offering. Not to teach. Not to declare. Not to advise.

No – just to share.

Share my journey of learning. Share my journey of living. Emotional intelligence, as it unfolded.

Through real, lived moments. Through quiet breakthroughs and loud mistakes.

But if I'm honest, sharing this journey has been anything but easy. Because it's meant speaking about things I'd much rather leave unsaid. It's also meant exposing the softer parts of myself – the ones that... still bruise easily. It means letting strangers see my flaws, my contradictions, the moments I fell flat. And making peace with the fact that some out there may be judging me, and my choices.

Hey, but that's okay.

Isn't that the first step of being emotionally intelligent?

If I can't walk my path openly – even when others have their opinions and still make space for those opinions without needing to defend myself... then maybe I haven't really learnt that much at all.

With that in mind – this is me, showing up. As I am. No neat ending. Just a real story, with rough edges, soft landings, and a lot of figuring-it-out along the way.

I share it in the quiet hope that maybe, just maybe, it speaks to something in you too.

Chapter 1:
The Quesadilla of Mind

Emotional Intelligence. It seems that this term was born not that far back in time – in 1964 – and it gained popularity even more recently when Daniel Goleman had an affair with it in 1995.

Emotional intelligence centres around two key capacities: **Personal Excellence** – the ability to understand and manage oneself – and **Social Excellence** – the ability to connect with, understand, and positively influence others.

I believe the concept has existed since time immemorial; only the official naming ceremony happened later. Much like that delicious dish my mother would conjure from leftover rotis (Indian round bread) and vegetables in our modest Indian kitchen, which years later I saw on the menu of a Mexican restaurant in Mumbai – and it had a handsome name: *Quesadilla!*

Indian philosophical thought also speaks about emotional intelligence. In the *Bhagavad Gita,* the emotionally intelligent person is called a *Sthithapragnya* – one who remains balanced amid joy and sorrow, unshaken by praise or calamity, and who can engage or disengage emotionally at will.

Since eternity, humans have used self-control and empathy to maintain relationships and extract the best out of themselves as well as others – the skills that form the pillars of emotional intelligence.

EQ, or **Emotional Quotient**, is a measure of emotional intelligence. Daniel Goleman, in his book *Emotional Intelligence: Why It Can Matter More Than IQ,* asserts that success in life and the workplace depends more – 80% more, in fact – on EQ than IQ. That's why people with sky-high IQs may falter in life, while those rich in EQ often thrive.

The good news? EQ can be developed at any age, unlike IQ, which is largely fixed at birth. Even better: humans are social animals – we develop and display emotional skills naturally, even intuitively.

If you've ever watched someone calm a panicked crowd, defuse an argument without authority, or persuade with empathy rather than force, you've seen emotional intelligence in action. Often, these people never took a course in it. So how did they learn?

Much like my mother, who didn't know what a quesadilla was but instinctively created something delicious, guided by purpose – saving food – she knew how to create flavour.

Similarly, when we are motivated to save a relationship or a situation, we instinctively apply emotional skills. We may not name it, but we live it. As Shakespeare said, "A rose is a rose is a rose." Its fragrance precedes its name – and does not depend on it.

PERSONAL EXCELLENCE

Chapter 2: Laying the Foundation, The Two Pillars

The intuitive nature of emotional intelligence is revealed in everyday behaviour. We avoid asking our boss for time off when they're angry. We use gentler tones with a colleague who seems low. We *sense,* and we *respond.*

It is gauging the emotion and choosing the action and/or best response. However, since the choice is *instinctive rather than conscious,* we may not do that all the time, and worse, when it is most required, i.e. when our own emotions run high.

Does that mean if we sharpen our instincts, we will be more emotionally intelligent?

Actually, yes!

But can we do that? Aren't instincts like God-given gifts?

One may be surprised! The truth is that instincts can actually be sharpened. I learned this from a colleague during my early days as a software engineer.

We were managing a high-stakes financial system, which was responsible for computing people's stock investment amounts and printing the dividend certificates. (*Yes! It was those days when demat accounts did not exist and physical certificates were posted!!*). Since the program tackled money – and huge amounts of it – no software error was excused. We had to be on high alert and swift to respond if any issues were reported.

On more than one occasion, this colleague predicted when and where something could go wrong, and it helped us to respond promptly, control the damage, and/or even evade it proactively.

It seemed like she had special powers!

Impressed as well as curious (and perhaps also envious), I finally asked her one day, "How do you do that? You are gifted with amazing intuition!"

She smiled and replied, "What you call intuition is actually acute awareness and active thinking. When you stay mindful, patterns become clear."

This became my first explicit lesson in emotional intelligence: ***Conscious Awareness.***

Much more than you are able to correlate the successfully handled situations to using emotional intelligence, I think you will be able to correlate the unsuccessfully handled situations to not being able to use emotional intelligence –

When you felt such anger that you blurted a harsh opinion and jeopardized your relationship… when you were reeling with sorrow and gave up that once-in-a-lifetime opportunity to build your career… when you surrendered to temptation in that moment of ecstasy and reset your diet…

The point I wish to make is that, more often than not, we all *know* what the right thing is. If we were giving someone advice, it probably would be foolproof. *Yet*, when we are in the moment, our emotions blur our prudence.

I use the 'baby bath' example on multiple occasions to explain the connection between conscious awareness and emotional intelligence:

If I accidentally touch something hot, I reflexively pull away. The initial feeling is of shock. After this moment of shock passes, rational thinking begins. That is when I actually assess whether the heat was bearable or brutal, and based on this conscious knowledge, I take the next action. I may decide that I can hold the object safely or that I need to wait/ use a holding aide.

Now, if I have to prepare a baby bath, I *have* to test the temperature of the water, for which I *have* to touch something hot. How do I go about it?

I pre-emptively activate rational thinking. I use my knowledge and previous experience to estimate an approximate temperature of the water based on appearance, how long the water heater has been turned on, etc.

This is precisely the conscious awareness which promotes emotional intelligence – Being aware of the possibilities and thus being prepared so we stay in control and respond to situations rather than become blurred as a consequence of being taken aback.

If only we are able to predict a situation, we can plan our action. Imagine… never being caught off guard, no regretful reactions, only pre-meditated responses.

Wow, right?

I may amuse a child when I tell, without being anywhere near the bathtub, whether the baby can be dipped into the tub.

Prediction. Intuition. It may seem like a special ability. However, it is a result of my conscious awareness.

Unlocking Beliefs: The Path to Conscious Awareness

Once, when my daughter was barely five years, I threw a tantrum in front of her. I genuinely believe that we, adults, throw more tantrums in front of our children than vice versa. In fact, I think, that is how they learn to throw tantrums.

Anyway, so here I was, flushed in face, shouting and slamming her notebook...

Because?

She couldn't tell me how to spell a simple five letter word even after my precious 15-minute effort.

Can you imagine how cruel I must have appeared to that little child? The lasting impact it had is obvious since she still remembers it in all clarity even through her adulthood.

God! I feel so ashamed of that now.

So why did I act that way?

If you had asked me about a decade back, I would have rattled off justifications:

I had so many other things to take care of; I had been patient for a long time; I gave her so many tips to remember the spelling; she obviously was not paying attention; she has to know the importance of education; she has to get disciplined... blah, blah, blah.

And I would not have been lying. This is what I actually believed then.

Belief. Something perceived as true, real.

Real? So, not an illusion.

But what is reality if not an illusion of an individual mind?

I am not trying to be poetic or ambiguous, just trying to stretch the envelope of your belief system. Because when that happens, perceptions change. That is what happened to me.

"Honesty is the best policy."

Heard it?

Believe it?

All those who conduct themselves honestly perhaps believe so. It is, after all, the creed of life, passed on through ancestral hands.

Let's be honest(!), most of our core beliefs are passed on to us through generations. Tried and tested 'truths' as they would call them and thus, we just accept them on face value.

A lot of these beliefs cannot be put to test without taking unreasonable risk anyway so we do not have much option. I mean, one will have to lead a whole life dishonestly to prove whether it is as fulfilling or not and that's a substantial lifetime risk to put it mildly!

However. We ought to be careful about what we believe in because it orchestrates our existence, our lives.

Imagine yourself sitting by a café window, quietly sipping your tea (or coffee, if that's more your thing), admiring the view outside. There's a tree in the distance, its branches ablaze with deep red flowers—so vivid they almost glow.

As you soak in the beauty, your gaze drifts to the next table, where a friendly face meets yours. Feeling a spark of connection, you smile and say, "Aren't those red flowers stunning? Do you happen to know what kind of tree that is?"

The person looks out of the window. You expect a shared moment of delight. But instead, there's a pause—and then a puzzled expression.

"I'm not sure what you mean. I don't see any tree. There's a small pile of dried leaves, though. I was wondering why that's there."

Now it's your turn to frown.

"What? It's right there! The flowers are so bright—how could you not see them?"

Frustration rises. Are they blind or something?

But then you get up and walk over to their side of the table. You look out through their window—and suddenly it makes sense.

From their angle, the tree is hidden. What you could see so clearly through your window was completely obscured from theirs.

Our beliefs are like those window frames. through which we look at the world. We each look out at the world through a unique frame, shaped by our experiences, values, upbringing, and expectations. What we see becomes our truth—our version of reality. Our perception of reality.

If I believe in God, I may see divine presence everywhere—and wonder why others are blind to it. If I don't, I might view those who do as misguided or delusional.

If it weren't for perception, we'd all see the exact same things when we look out. But we don't.

What feels modern to me may seem disrespectful to you.

What you value deeply might seem trivial to me.

The world hasn't changed. Only the window has. And depending on how it seems to me - I respond.

Now, let me revisit my tantrum incident with my daughter.

Did I truly believe that not being able to spell a five-letter word in kindergarten would jeopardize my daughter's entire educational future?

Of course not.

What I did believe was that education matters – and I wanted my daughter to share that belief. I wanted her to give her best to learning, to take it seriously, to care as much as I did.

Further, did I believe she was being manipulative or careless – deliberately ignoring my efforts?

Absolutely not.

She was in tears, clearly trying. Clearly distressed.

So, a fair and more accurate conclusion would be this: something was obstructing her ability to learn in that moment.

When I piece it all together, here's what emerges:

"I believed that education is important, and I wanted my daughter to value it and give her best. I knew she wasn't a careless or manipulative child, so if she couldn't learn, something must have been in the way – something I failed to understand."

Just saying it aloud, makes me realize whether I was angry because she couldn't spell the word or because I couldn't understand what was obstructing her.

This realization is conscious awareness.

Awareness of the emotion I feel, and the belief that fuels it.

My happiness, my sorrow, my anger – all my emotions. They shape how I act, how I respond. And at their core lies my perception: the way I interpret a situation. My perception which is rooted in my beliefs.

If I hadn't believed that education was important – or more specifically, that performing well in exams mattered – I wouldn't have felt even a flicker of anger in that moment.

Which makes it clear: it wasn't really about my daughter at all.

It was about me. All along.

My second lesson in emotional intelligence - Self Responsibility.

Conscious awareness and Self Responsibility.

These form the two pillars of emotional intelligence – the foundation upon which personal excellence is built.

Chapter 3: Knowledge Vs Knowing, The Hidden Gap

Knowledge, by itself, does not make one accomplished.

We're constantly surrounded by teachers and mentors – each passing on precious life lessons - some intentional, others tacit or accidental. Like players in a game of 'pass the ball,' if we're paying attention, we catch these offerings. And yet, most of the time, they seem to make little difference.

At least, that's what I realized in hindsight.

Pearls of wisdom like *conscious awareness* and *self-responsibility* were handed to me – but I just tucked them away in the corners of my mind. I didn't do anything with them. Not until life made them impossible to ignore.

And yet, looking back, I don't believe that I – or anyone else – is foolish or careless in letting them sit idle. We don't reject wisdom because we are blind to its value. We often set it aside because, at that moment, we believe we already possess all we need.

Our personal beliefs – our own carefully gathered pearls – often feel perfect just as they are. We become deeply attached to them, convinced they need no revision or addition. In fact, we interpret the world in ways that reinforce this sense of adequacy, subtly affirming the sufficiency of our existing wisdom.

In essence, we are convinced of who we are – until life, in one way or another, challenges that conviction.

Sometimes, this disruption comes through struggle – when our current version of self no longer works, no longer copes, no longer feels aligned. Other times, if we're fortunate, we encounter someone whose presence shifts something in us – someone whose being quietly urges us to grow.

More often than not, it's a combination of both.

Like everyone else, I have lived through many versions of myself. Some transformations were inspired by admiration – a desire to become more like *that* someone who stirred something noble or brave within me. Others were born out of disappointment, loss, or failure – signs that my old ways had outlived their usefulness.

At the time of my daughter's spelling incident, I was utterly convinced that my outburst – my tantrum – was justified.

Just as any tantrum-throwing child believes theirs is. And so, such tantrums kept recurring, disguised as "appropriate" behaviour for a so-called *perfect* mother raising a *wholesome* child.

Until one day.

As part of our routine, I would drop my daughter off at school every morning and pick her up in the afternoon. That morning, as I walked her to the school gate, a security guard asked me to leave the premises and not linger near the entrance until my child was out of my sight.

My ego bristled. I felt dismissed, even disrespected.

So I reacted – loudly and emotionally. Right there on school grounds, I began scolding him, insisting he learn some manners.

The irony, of course, was painful.

But what followed was worse.

That afternoon, when I returned to pick up my daughter, she broke into tears the moment she saw me. Through sobs, she confessed she had spent the whole day terrified – afraid the guard might shoot me with his gun… or that her teacher might punish *her* for her mother's behaviour.

That moment pierced me.

This little girl – my little girl – not only sensed that her mother's behaviour was wrong, but also believed *she* would be held accountable for it. That *she* would bear the punishment for my conduct.

There I was, trying so hard to be the perfect role model – and instead, I was becoming her source of fear… and shame.

From that moment on, I began to pay closer attention to how I was behaving. It felt a bit like stepping back into my teenage years – that hyper-awareness of being watched, of needing to *appear* a certain way at all times. Except now, my idea of "looking a certain way" had evolved far beyond styled hair and carefully chosen outfits.

This was the beginning of my journey into conscious awareness.

I know the term carries a spiritual resonance – and perhaps some of you will connect with that. But the truth is, conscious awareness doesn't have to begin with a profound awakening. It can start small. Very small.

It's a bit like being told to "be positive," and asking, "But how?" And the response is simply, "Start by smiling."

A smile, on the surface, is just a facial expression – and to *put one on* can feel artificial, even forced. But here's the beauty: the very act of smiling triggers the release of calming hormones in the brain. These hormones uplift our mood, which leads to more genuine positivity... which in turn, leads to a more natural smile. And so the cycle begins.

In much the same way, I found that mindfulness – when practiced consistently – grows into something deeply rewarding. Even if it starts off feeling mechanical or superficial, it eventually becomes a lived experience. A way of being.

When I began seeing myself with objectivity, a sense of caution awakened. It became easier to regulate my behaviour when I could envision how my actions might appear to others, what impact they might have, and what consequences might unfold once the moment had passed.

I discovered ***self-control.***

Self-control is a very fascinating toy! It gives us the reason to pause - and that pause makes all the difference. Difference between reaction and response - impulsive reactions and *pre-meditated* responses... regret and resolution

As someone who has long loved Bollywood and dabbled in acting, I understood the dramatic weight of a pause on stage – its power to hold attention, to shift emotion, to elevate meaning. What I hadn't yet realized was how equally transformative those pauses could be **off** the stage – in the real-life theatre of relationships, choices, and inner conflict.

The **pause**, I discovered, is a super-tool of conscious awareness.

At first, I used it to reflect on how I wanted to come across in a particular situation or with a particular person – and then to notice whether I was, in fact, aligning with that intention. Slowly, I began to regulate my responses, choosing behaviour that was more aligned with my deeper values than with momentary emotional impulses.

And once I saw how powerfully these pauses were enhancing my "performance," I began creating space for more of them.

Soon, the pause was no longer just about post-behaviour reflection. It became a space for introspection. I paused to ask *why* I was feeling a certain way, behaving in a certain way – or not behaving in ways I wished I could. I began observing others, too – their moods, their silences, their overreactions – and wondered what lay beneath *their* surface.

Unconsciously, I was shifting from a reactive mode to a proactive one.

Unknowingly, I was sharpening what we call *intuition.*

The first few pauses helped me become aware of how I was feeling.
The next few helped me act rather than react – and avoid regret.
But it was the deeper series of pauses that invited me to ask

why I was feeling what I was feeling. These were the pauses that challenged the beliefs I held about myself and the world.

This was the turning point – the shift from believing I already possessed all the pearls of wisdom I would ever need, to reassessing their value… and making room for new ones.

I began expanding my wisdom, rather than being limited by it.

They say that doubting oneself is a sign of weakness or low competence. But I'm not so sure anymore. In fact, I've come to believe that never offering the benefit of doubt, including to yourself – is far more restrictive.

Doubt can be a doorway. It leads to inquiry.

Inquiry fosters understanding. And understanding is the soil in which true growth takes root.

My journey of conscious self-awareness began the moment I doubted what I thought I knew. Gradually, I began to *know* what I had only assumed I knew.

Today, I stand by the words of Nicolaus Copernicus:

"To know that we know what we know, and to know that we do not know what we do not know – that is true knowledge."

Chapter 4: Self-responsibility, Freedom of Acceptance

True knowledge is not restrictive. It does not set boundaries. There is no set 'module' that completes the course.

Vast, endless ocean with many parts unexplored at any given time….

And we have to swim in it.

At first, the idea of not knowing everything feels unsettling. We are conditioned to strive for perfection, to be 'toppers,' to always have the right answer. The prospect of revealing something uncomfortable about ourselves – to ourselves – is even more daunting.

However, it became worthwhile when I experienced the joy of freedom which comes with accepting something without judgement.

As I began to observe myself objectively, I started to recognize how different people and situations impacted me. What made me happy. What left me anxious or angry.

This was stage one – the nascent stage of self-awareness.

I still justified and defended my emotions. It felt natural to blame others for my negative states. After all, why would anyone intentionally make themselves angry or sad?

So, in this phase, happiness came from two places:

- locating the 'culprits' for my pain (e.g., "how dumb people make me angry," "how unkindness makes me sad"), and
- taking full credit for my positive emotions (e.g., "how I controlled my temper," or "how I spread kindness").

I got better at identifying my emotional triggers and even developed strategies to avoid or neutralize them. For instance, as a self-confessed tidiness freak, I used to feel deeply frustrated watching someone create a mess in the kitchen while cooking. But conscious awareness helped me recognize the frustration before it took hold. I learned to avoid that moment altogether by staying out of the kitchen when I sensed it coming. It helped not only me, but also those around me. The emotional environment began to shift.

The journey so far felt rewarding. I was successfully exposing myself to more positive emotions than negative ones. I had started leaning into my strengths, and the resulting confidence uplifted my performance in life.

But then – something ironic began to happen.

The more I tasted happiness, the more I wanted to make it permanent. Instead of just avoiding triggers for negative emotions, my mind started searching for ways to eliminate them altogether.

This is when my ascend to next stage of emotional intelligence began.

I had become adept at keeping difficult conversations at bay – like not bringing up a sensitive topic with my husband that might spark conflict. Avoiding the discussion kept the sadness away... but only temporarily. The issue remained. The frustration returned.

Route to eternal peace has to pass through resolving our 'why's. I started investigating my *whys*.

Why was I getting angry? Why did certain moments make me sad? I began to reflect on my emotional highs and lows with meticulous curiosity. And slowly, the root cause emerged.

Behind my emotional upheavals, I discovered a single, powerful force: ***My* insecurity.**

For example: I'd get angry when my children spent more time playing than studying. But why? Because I feared they might fail. And why did that scare me? Because I saw their failure as *my* failure as a mother.

So I wasn't afraid that *they* would fail – I was afraid *I* would fail.

No matter how much I tried to shift the blame, the truth was undeniable. I – and I alone – was responsible for how I felt.

Holding the hand of conscious awareness, I arrived at **self-responsibility**.

To be self-responsible meant no one else had the power to make me feel anything. Not without my permission. I had the *power*. Which meant I had the *choice*.

A choice to feel one way or another. To react immediately or to pause and reflect. To spiral into anger or respond with composure. This awareness – this *agency* – was remarkable.

As I questioned my feelings more deeply, my search turned inward. I ventured into the darkest, most hidden corners of my own psyche.

And yes – it was terrifying.

Sometimes I felt like a selfish, fragile soul. But the deeper I went, the more I discovered that I just deemed these corners dark and so never cared (or dared) to get here but they had hidden wealth.

It was like riding a rollercoaster. Midway through, the stomach drops, fear screams – and you curse the decision to get on. But when you reach the end, exhilaration washes over you. And you feel… victorious.

In those dark corners, I found treasure chests.

Each one was locked with a chain of *whys*. Each time I unlocked one, it revealed another within. But now I was curious enough to continue. Until the Whys cease... till the answers felt convincing and till they pointed towards *me*.

Here's one example of such an inner dialogue:

"I feel irritated with mess." Why?

"Because tidiness is good." Why?

"Because it's a great value." Why is it *your* value?

"Maybe because my mother always liked things tidy." That was *her* preference. Why is it yours?

"Actually… I think I don't want others to see me living or working in mess." Why?

"Because I want to be seen as perfect." Why does that matter?

And then – the memory surfaces.

"My father, though loving, was acutely critical of my mother. I sought his approval. Maybe that's where the subconscious drive to appear flawless ('hide' any mess) came from."

That's when I realized: liking tidiness is fine. But becoming restless or guilty due to a childhood insecurity… is not.

My logical, adult self knows that expecting flawlessness is unrealistic. And that insight was liberating.

The sparkle from these treasure chests illuminated dark corners. I was no longer afraid to visit them. I began to see that some of our emotions come not from the present moment, but from unprocessed pasts. Sometimes, even grief is a conditioned response – something we *think* we're supposed to feel, and then feel guilty when we don't.

But once I understood the *why*, I had a choice.

I could continue feeling and acting the same way – or I could choose differently, from a place of awareness, not fear.

I saw myself clearly: not as someone perfect, or broken – but simply… human.

I may not be as good as some people think. But I'm also not as flawed as I sometimes fear. I am *me*. And that is enough.

Freedom came not from perfection, but from acceptance.

I am not perfect.

But I am OK.

And now – I have the choice to be whoever I wish to be.

Chapter 5: Emotions, The Invisible Strings

Puppetry is one of the most ancient and vibrant art forms in India. As a child, I remember watching many *gully* (street) puppet shows – spellbound as those lifeless dolls danced with such charm. The puppeteer, hidden behind the curtain, pulled the strings while the puppets seemed to move entirely on their own.

Emotions act as that puppeteer for us.

They reside beneath the surface, tucked beneath thought and language, quietly tugging the strings of our reactions, choices, and impulses. We may imagine ourselves as autonomous – rational, self-directed beings – yet more often than not, it is emotion that moves the hand before we think, shapes the tone before we speak, decides the retreat or confrontation before we've weighed the consequences.

Fear may freeze the body before logic deems it necessary. Anger may drive the voice to rise, the fist to clench, the door to slam – all before reflection arrives.

At any given moment, we may experience a mix of emotions. For instance, when finishing school, I might feel excited to begin a new job in a different city, but also sad to leave my family behind. These feelings don't cancel each other out – they coexist, sometimes even intensifying one another. Yet, even when emotions share the stage, one of them often edges forward into the spotlight. It becomes slightly louder, heavier, more persuasive. And that dominant emotion becomes the driver of our decision.

So, in my example, if the thrill of independence outweighs the pain of separation, I take the job. If the sorrow of leaving home looms larger, I decline the offer. The puppeteer doesn't just pull one string – it tests the tension in all of them, then follows the strongest pull.

Emotional intelligence is our ability to recognize, understand, and manage these emotions – instead of letting them manage us. The higher our emotional intelligence (EQ), the more influence we have over our own reactions, even in emotionally intense situations.

Personal excellence is built on two core strengths – conscious awareness and self-control. With conscious awareness we begin to recognize the strings. With self-responsibility and self-control, we learn when to follow their pull, and when to resist. We can become conscious co-authors of our movement, rather than blind performers. In that moment, the puppeteer becomes not a tyrant, but a dance partner.

But before we begin to recognize the strings, let us first and foremost understand that not everything we feel is an emotion.

A racing heart might be caused by caffeine, not fear. A restless mind could stem from boredom, not anxiety. Physical sensations, thoughts, moods, and even instinctual reactions often masquerade as emotions, though they are not the same.

What is true emotion?

We often list emotions like joy, sorrow, love, hate, anger, fear, shame, or disgust. But neuroscience suggests that not all of these are emotions in the strictest sense. According to recent research by Dr. Vrticka at the University of Essex (UK), there are only four **basic emotions** that are biologically hardwired into us:

- **Angust** (a blend of anger and disgust, with anger as the primary emotion)
- **Fearprise** (a blend of fear and surprise, where fear is the dominant emotion)
- **Happiness**
- **Sadness**

These core emotions are universal, presumed to be hardwired (present from birth rather than learned) and physiologically distinctive.

Disgust is like anger. While anger often leads to direct confrontation and a desire to correct or punish, disgust tends to produce indirect responses – like withdrawal or avoidance.

Similarly, fear and surprise have been grouped together because our body's initial response to surprise mimics fear. What follows – relief, joy, or sorrow – depends on the nature of the surprise. As Dr. Vrticka puts it, fear can be seen as "negatively valenced surprise."

All other named emotions – irritation, anxiety, excitement, embarrassment – are variations or blends of these core four.

For instance, fear can range from mild unease to full-blown terror; anger can span from annoyance to rage. These are emotional gradients, not distinct emotions in themselves.

It's important to remember that emotions are **organic** – they are chemical and physiological responses to stimuli. They arise instinctively. If left unmanaged, their physiological effects can harm us but no emotion is inherently bad; it can be negative or positive depending on what energy it generates.

That's where emotional intelligence steps in – to help us notice, accept, and evaluate our emotions before they dictate our actions.

We begin by **acknowledging** what we're feeling. Then we **accept** the emotion – without judgment – as a natural response. Finally, we ask: *Do I need to temper this emotion? Or is it valid and useful as it is?*

Interestingly, many things we call "emotions" aren't emotions at all.

Take love and hate, for example. These are **sentiments** – sustained attitudes of mind. Sentiments are long-term. Emotion is instinctive and is triggered by situational cues and physiological responses A woman may *love* her husband (sentiment) even while feeling deeply *annoyed* (emotion) at him in a specific moment.

Or consider hunger. We say, "I *feel* hungry," but hunger is a **sensation**, not an emotion – it signals a biological need for food.

Then there are reactions we mistake for emotions but are actually **thoughts or interpretations** – cognitive assessments influenced by culture, upbringing, or social context.

For example: *humiliation.* We say we feel humiliated, but this is a conclusion we draw after interpreting someone's behaviour. The underlying emotion may be anger – perhaps directed at ourselves for not living up to a personal or social ideal.

Because our brains process all this so quickly, these thoughts *feel* like emotions. But they are often reflections of deeper belief systems, not instinctual reactions.

By becoming aware of the fundamental emotions, and learning to identify them underneath our thoughts, we begin to take back control. We can look beyond the surface and ask better questions of ourselves.

And that's the journey I now invite you on – to operate on these fundamental emotions, understand their architecture, and explore what truly moves you… and why.

Chapter 6:
Anger, Nature's Gift

When I began to be self-aware, I realised that every time I felt anger, it was rooted in my own insecurity, my own fear.

Whether it was irritation when the air conditioner broke down just before bedtime (*and I feared a sleepless night in heat*), or the defensiveness I felt when someone asked how my struggling project was going (it wasn't the question that upset me. It was the fear: *What if I can't resolve it?*

There is fear beneath irritation or anger, even when it's triggered by something seemingly trivial like someone's mannerisms. Fear of losing control - that our environment isn't fully within our control.

That's when I started a personal ritual. Whenever I felt angry, I would pause and gently ask myself, "what are you afraid of?"

Biology Behind the Emotion

My theory is that anger is nature's gift to us - to defend ourselves in any danger situation. It is clear when we look closely at what happens in the body during anger:

- **Adrenaline floods the system**, making us alert and energized. Adrenalin makes us feel confident/ready to take risks.
- **Heart rate increases** causing more oxygen to be released into the blood.
- **Blood oxygen rises** and rushes to our limbs (hands/legs) – hence the flushed face, enabling the limbs to take one of the two actions required in any danger situation - ***Fight or Flight.***

It's the exact mechanism a prey needs when threatened by a predator. Instinctively, when our brain perceives a threat – be it physical, emotional, or social – this ancient alarm bell rings. The response is automatic.

I witnessed this on the road one day.

Two cars narrowly avoided a collision – both drivers slammed their brakes just in time. In seconds, they leapt out of their vehicles, slamming doors, voices raised, tempers flaring.

They hadn't been physically harmed. But in that brief, heart-stopping moment, they had come face to face with the possibility of losing their lives – the most deeply held instinctive fear. That brush with danger was enough to jolt their brains into high alert, triggering the primal response we recognize as **anger**.

It wasn't rage for rage's sake. It was fear, dressed in fury.

But, while our physiology hasn't changed much since the Neanderthal era, our lives have. Our needs have evolved. Hence a primitive response to all threats may not be appropriate.

We need to, therefore, train our brain to emerge out of its neanderthal instincts.

The Value-Anger Equation

The greater the value we place on something, the more intense our reaction when it's threatened.

Imagine this:

You're waiting in a long queue to submit a form.

- If the weather is pleasant, the long wait may at most be just slightly irritable.
- Add sweltering heat, and the discomfort grows – your patience shortens. Annoyance grows.
- Now imagine the counter may close before your turn – your anxiety builds which quickly turns to frustration. You may protest and shout if someone cuts in line.

- And finally, if that form secures admission to your dream college, and someone cuts in line, near the closing hour of the counter – your anger may explode.

Same situation, different intensity – all depending on how much is at stake for *you*.

The core trigger? Fear within you. And therefore, Control is also within you.

When we try to find these triggers outside us and blame - the weather, the system, the person- we *pass the control to make us feel better* to them. Since they cannot fix what we feel, we continue to feel miserable.

The Blame Game: Why We Stay Angry

Too often, we pass the onus of *our bad habits* to other people or circumstances - *"Yes, I smoke – but it's my friend's influence."*

We project ourselves as a victim to avoid taking any blame or be responsible for any corrective action. Shortfall of this approach is that we trade ownership for helplessness. If the cause lies outside us, we're powerless. *When the onus lies with my friend, there is nothing I can do to save my lungs.*

We do the same with anger - *"I lost my temper – but he made me angry."*

Have you ever seen a street dog barking at a man with a stick, who's carrying it only because *he* is afraid of the dog?

Citing anger as a response to someone else's anger is like that.

Fear, Anger, and the Battle Loop

Anger evolves from fear.

Fear activates our instinct to defend, and that defence takes the shape of anger. When this anger sparks a 'fight' response, it manifests as an attack – aimed at the perceived source of threat. The moment the other person feels attacked, *their* fear is triggered, prompting *their* anger as a defence.

I use a simple exercise in my workshops. I ask:

"Do you ever get angry for no reason at all?"
The answer is always: *Never.*

Then I ask:

"If your anger always has a reason, why do you assume someone else's anger is unreasonable?"

That usually lands hard.

It's ironic – when we see someone scared, we instinctively offer comfort and reassurance. But when that same fear grows into anger, we tend to react to the aggression rather than the vulnerability beneath it. Anger is fear reshaped, yet instead of empathizing, we defend ourselves – and miss the cry for understanding hidden within the outburst.

But imagine if, instead of reacting, we paused and asked, *"What is this person scared of?"*

"How can I reassure them instead of attacking back?"

The Power of the Pause

Two simple realizations changed my life:

- My anger is triggered by my fear.
- Other people's anger is also rooted in their fear.

This helped me *feel* anger less often, *handle* it more consciously and be more tolerant of others' anger. But anger didn't disappear – nor should it.

Because anger, when understood and directed, is a gift.

When Anger Is Valid – and Valuable

Anger equips us to respond in moments of perceived threat. If we pause to evaluate the danger – and understand the fear beneath it – we gain the power to choose our response wisely. Some situations call for confrontation. Others are best avoided. And many, upon reflection, may not warrant anger at all.

One day, someone in a social WhatsApp group casually criticized a recent film by my favourite actor. Instantly, I felt the urge to jump in and defend them.

But I paused – and asked myself, gently, "*Why are you feeling annoyed?*"

The first answer surfaced quickly: "*Because he's a brilliant actor! Clearly, they don't appreciate the craft!*"

But I've trained myself to continue the inquiry – not to stop until the answer involves *I, me, or myself*. So, I kept digging.

Eventually, I reached the truth:

"*I feel annoyed because my choices reflect who I am. When someone criticizes my preference, I interpret it as a criticism of me. That feels like a personal slight – and that perceived threat activates my instinct to defend.*"

Once I understood that – I could pause. Reflect. And remind myself: Others' opinions are not threats. They're perspectives.

Everyone is entitled to their opinion – including me. Others' views need not feel like personal attacks. In fact, they might offer a perspective I've overlooked due to my emotional bias.

I don't have to agree. But I can be open.

In this case, the anger wasn't warranted. It was rooted in fear – and once acknowledged, it dissolved.

Of course, not all situations are like this. Sometimes our fear – and the anger it triggers – is justified. There are moments when injustice or real threat must be confronted.

In such moments, emotional intelligence doesn't mean suppressing anger. It means channelling it consciously – not to provoke fear in others, but to inspire meaningful change.

In one of my sessions, a participant shared this:

"I've never faced gender discrimination, but I feel a surge of anger when someone expresses narrow-minded views about women."

That was emotional intelligence in action. She had already achieved:

- Awareness of her emotion
- Acceptance without judgment

Next came understanding. I asked, "What are you scared of?"

When I asked her, she said, "B*ecause such sentiments lead to societal divide/conflicts ultimately impacting humanity negatively."*

"Still, why are *you* feeling so perturbed? What is *your* fear?" I asked.

Her answer eventually:

"I fear that such views, if left unchallenged, could limit my own opportunities and those of women I care about."

Valid. Her fear wasn't baseless.

Witnessing injustice often triggers fear – and this fear typically arises from two sources:

- We can imagine the injustice happening to us (empathy).
- We feel it threatens our core values (the need to defend personal beliefs).

The trickle of emotional energy feels like the damp heat of a sweat line near the ears. It builds restlessness, and soon, the anger demands an outlet.

Under that pressure, a person might lash out – arguing forcefully with someone who holds a conflicting view. But rarely does this lead to meaningful change. The other person, feeling their right to opinion attacked, becomes defensive. No one shifts their stance. The injustice remains unchallenged – and now, the relationship is strained too.

In an effort to protect that relationship, she might instead suppress her anger. But this only deepens the sense of helplessness. Repressed anger doesn't vanish – it simmers, feeding internal frustration and emotional fatigue.

What's needed is not suppression or aggression – but a conscious strategy that addresses the *root cause* of anger. In her case, it wasn't just disagreement with someone's views – it was a deeper sense of helplessness in the face of a widespread, ingrained belief system.

She was a blogger. What if she redirected that energy into writing? Persuasive, insightful articles that celebrate women's abilities and dismantle biases, one story at a time. By expressing her truth through thoughtful communication, she could feel empowered – and perhaps, even spark real change.

Anger is not to be detested as an emotion. If I do not feel compelled to protect *any* belief, then I am perhaps a person of questionably limited values and principles.

There are real injustices in the world. Times when anger is justified, even necessary. Exploitation will prevail. No revolutions would happen if anger completely vanished.

Anger is a gift – a powerful force granted to protect, energize, and propel us. But like any gift, its value lies in how we use it. When guided by awareness, it can uplift our lives; when left unchecked, it can unravel them.

The key to unlocking its wisdom lies in our greatest inner tool: the pause.

Don't explode. Don't suppress. Pause. Ask:

- What am I afraid of?
- Is that fear justified?
- What's the best way to protect myself or create change?

This pause acts like a riverbed – guiding the flow of anger. Without it, anger is a broken pipe, flooding everything in its path. With it, anger becomes a stream of purpose – nourishing change.

Ironically, taking pause is the remedy to calm the fears and yet, *fear is the reason why we fail to pause.*

Chapter 7: Fear, Acquired Burden

Since the discussion on anger often refers to fear, let me share what I've come to understand about it. The deeper I delved, the clearer it became: if anger is nature's gift, then fear is the burden we've learned to carry.

A burden so potent, so deeply woven into our choices, that it seems to drive almost everything we do.

"There's me that you see
Then there's me that I do
But further deep, there's a me
That even myself dreads to view
Dark desires interlaced with fears
Buried there, yet continue to brew
And as much as I deny,
They are the ones
Who make me do, what I do!"

What is fear?

Google defines it as, "an unpleasant emotion caused by the threat of danger, pain, or harm". The keyword here is 'threat'. Not the actual danger, pain, or harm – but the *possibility* of it. Fear is a proactive emotion born from imagination, from assumptions. It's not always rooted in reality.

I fear my child may fail or that my boss may not promote me or, that my spouse might be unfaithful. These things may not be happening – and may never happen – yet my mind races ahead, simulating their consequences as if they already were.

Left unchecked, this imagined threat begins to feel real. The result is - I start to act how I would have acted if danger/pain/harm was real. My defence mechanism, which is anger, is activated. Leaving my child or boss or spouse confused by a storm they never saw coming.

There's a powerful acronym that captures this well:

F.E.A.R. - False Evidence Appearing Real.

Where Does Fear Begin?

Fear is an organic emotion implying it is present from birth. The first fear we absorb is the fear of survival. We don't just need to judge but also *anticipate* any threat to our survival. The foetus claims nourishment from the mother, instinctively prioritizing its own growth. Once born, we continue to seek and protect everything vital to survival.

In our earliest human forms, survival meant detecting predators. An accurate judgement of predators kept us protected. We evolved to read threats in rustling bushes and unfamiliar eyes.

But modern humans have expanded our definition of survival: now it includes social belonging, influence, emotional fulfilment, even comfort. Today's "predators" are often abstract – rejection, failure, loneliness, insignificance.

People say hatred is the root of evil. But why do we hate? Isn't it when we *believe* someone threatens us, our loved ones, our beliefs, our environment? Isn't hatred rooted in fear?

Some argue selfishness is the root of evil. But again, why are we selfish? Because we're afraid – afraid that someone might take away our happiness, our peace. At its core, *fear* is the common denominator.

Swami Vivekananda once said, "*It is fear that is the great cause of misery in the world.*" I agree. Anger, jealousy, hatred, greed – they are all children of fear.

So How Do We Stop Being Fearful?

In ancient times, we had to detect threats to our physical life. Now, we must also protect abstract things: our identities, our reputations, our dreams. This multiplication of things to guard has amplified our fear. The more we have to protect, the more we scan for threats – and the more vulnerable we feel.

We become hyper-alert: avoiding someone rumoured to be rude, withholding trust after witnessing betrayal, doubting our success based on gender or class stereotypes.

But here's the paradox: *our fear isn't born from the threat itself.* It's born from a *lack of faith* in our ability to handle that threat. It's not the danger that unravels us – it's the belief that we won't survive it.

It is not the stimulus but the inability to deal with the stimulus. If I trust that I can manage financial loss, I won't fear poverty. If I know how to call pest control, pests don't scare me. If I believe I can live joyfully alone, betrayal doesn't terrify me.

So, to dissolve fear, we must shift focus: from *removing threats* to *strengthening ourselves.*

That will strengthen our faith to deal with threats.

Faith Is the Antidote

"Faith and fear both demand you believe in something you cannot see. You choose."

Recognizing potential risks is wise – like knowing a knife can cause harm. My parents taught me that early on and didn't allow me to handle one until I was ready. But I can't let that awareness sabotage me. I can't go through life banning knives or assuming that anyone holding one intends to hurt me. That kind of fear distorts reality – it leads to paranoia, not protection.

Faith is not about religion. It is a belief. Belief that

- Things may not be as bad as they seem and
- That whatever happens, I can handle it.

Some draw this from belief in a higher power, others from confidence in their own resilience. Either way, faith is what guards our sanity while keeping us alert.

I don't outlaw knives because they *can* hurt. I teach myself how to use them safely. Similarly, I don't banish risk from life – I learn how to navigate it wisely.

Be aware of the risks but not be averse to them by default; Assess people but not be suspicious of them by default; Be wary but not be scared by default.

Emotional intelligence gives us that power.

Our past experiences shape our perceptions. We use those perceptions – sometimes inherited second-hand from what we've seen, heard, or read – to interpret the present.

Experiences → Beliefs → Perceived Reality

If experiences are unchangeable, does that mean our reality is fixed?

Not quite – but believing so can limit us. It narrows the range of what we believe is possible. Just because I've never seen, heard, or read about an ocean doesn't mean it doesn't exist.

So how do we expand what we believe is possible?

By adding *emotional intelligence* to the equation.

Experiences + Emotional Intelligence → Beliefs → Perceived Reality

Emotional intelligence gives us power to reshape the beliefs that define our reality.

Imagine this power! The power to create a reality not bound by the past but expanded by insight.

With emotional intelligence, I can begin to challenge my assumptions. I might say, "Yes, that mushroom made me sick once – but maybe it wasn't the mushroom. Maybe it was just my stomach that day. Let me try again." I can stop avoiding pizza over a single bad experience.

I can let go of the bias that tells me not to trust the new colleague just because she's fashionable – as if caring about one's appearance somehow disqualifies someone from being responsible or competent. Emotional intelligence helps me see that style doesn't negate substance.

I can stop fearing that something *will* go wrong just because it *once* did – or because it *seems* like it might.

Emotional Intelligence motivates me to take a pause.

I learn to pause, reflect, and respond with clarity rather than assumption. Rationalize my thoughts before I perceive something as absolute threat. To view a situation not just from our narrow window, but from others' perspectives too. To consider: "What else might be true here?"

Remember What Truly Matters

Ironically, *being alive* – the root of all needs – is often missing from our survival list. We take it for granted. We act like the monkey who chooses a banana over a $100 bill, unaware of the greater value.

Mental and physical well-being are the foundations on which everything else stands. A fragile mind invites anxiety; a frail body can't fight. Emotional intelligence motivates me to take responsibility – to nurture our resilience. Responsibility to strengthen my capabilities to effectively confront the threat, even in the event of worst-case scenario.

That means:

- **Building a strong support system** through meaningful relationships
- **Sustaining mental and physical health** through self-care
- **Sharpening skills** through continuous personal growth

"I cheated on my fear, broke up with my doubt, got engaged to faith and now I am married to my dream" - Anonymous.

Chapter 8: Joy and Sorrow, Siamese twins

What Is Happiness?

The wise often say, *"Happiness is a state of mind, completely independent of external factors."*

While this definition may be accurate, it can feel vague – abstract and difficult to visualize, and hence, attain.

Yet, happiness is something we all seek. To make it more tangible, I decided to take a mathematical, structured approach. From what I had learned so far about emotional intelligence, I was able to derive four meaningful corollaries.

Corollary 1: If I can reduce the space for Anger, Fear and Sorrow, Joy will expand automatically.

Let's consider the four fundamental emotions: **Joy, Sorrow, Anger,** and **Fear.**

Poets describe the heart as the seat of emotions. Suppose we imagine the heart as a fixed container with four flexible compartments – one for each emotion. If one compartment grows, the others must shrink. This implies if I can shrink the space occupied by anger, fear, and sorrow, joy will naturally expand.

Hence, if I can reduce the compartment size of Anger, Fear and Sorrow, Joy will expand automatically.

We have already looked at anger and fear in depth. We have understood how emotional intelligence abilities empower a person to effectively regulate the size of these compartments. Ability to

- recognize the emotion (conscious awareness)
- Accept the emotion (Self-responsibility)
- Pause, reflect and then act (Self-control).

Rather than being consumed by an unpleasant emotion, we can pause and acknowledge it with compassion. Then we can choose a response that aligns with our deeper values.

Corollary 2: If I can control my attitude, I can control my happiness.

If happiness is truly independent of external factors, then it must arise from within – from that which is mine to govern.

What makes up a person?

- Physical features
- Skills and talents
- Attitude

Of these, physical features, though least in our control, are the easiest to alter.

Attitude, paradoxically, is entirely within our control but hardest to change.

Hence, if I can control my attitude, I will be able to control my happiness.

Our attitude is shaped by our beliefs and observations.

Emotional intelligence gives us the power to challenge the beliefs which are leading to feeling of unhappiness and observe situation from different perspectives.

Conscious awareness and self-control also enable us to shift our focus and engage in activities that we enjoy; boost our mood. Move from being helpless to in control.

Corollary 3: **To maintain happiness, reduce expectations of others and situations; instead, set goals for yourself.**

Returning to Corollary 1: if I am not sad, angry, or afraid – am I automatically happy?

Not quite. I've had many such moments where I wasn't particularly unhappy, but neither was I joyful. Something was missing.

On reflection, I found that happiness often emerged when expectations were fulfilled:

- When situations unfolded as hoped
- When people behaved as expected
- When I met goals, I had set for myself

I have limited control, if at all, over situations and people. However, I can regulate my expectations from myself.

Thus, *Corollary 3* follows as -

To keep control of my happiness, I should *reduce my expectation from others and situations. Instead, set goals for self.*

Professional goals, social goals, personal goals... Achievement goals, behavioural goals, health goals, skill goal... When I achieve these goals, I meet my expectations and feel happy.

This makes a lot of sense as I consider the fact that when I am not particularly sad or angry or fearful but also not really 'happy', I am actually feeling a kind of 'dullness'... ***What I am missing is 'purpose'.***

I need a purpose. *Not a task.* Just purpose.

Purpose could be 'rest'. After I have achieved the purpose, I am happy. Thereafter I need another purpose or I feel lost, dull. Purposeless day seems dull. This also explains why we find a lot of retired people, feeling dull... not unhappy in theory and yet not happy.

Purpose gives life meaning. Goals are milestones toward that purpose. When we pursue something meaningful, we are also less distracted by unmet external expectations. Purpose is not tied to task or means. It is greater than both. Therefore, it allows flexibility of approach; change of perspectives.

When we retain a purpose through sorrow, dullness does not persist. Pursuit of happiness continues.

Corollary 4: **Happiness is a milestone, not a destination.**

We often treat happiness like a distant goal – an eventuality to reach. But goals are fixed points in the future. Milestones, in contrast, are encountered along the way. If we view happiness as a milestone, we allow ourselves to experience it frequently, gently, presently.

Hence, Happiness should be like milestones, not a goal.

Happiness is not as unattainable as we are sometimes brought to think. Nor is it a dramatic crescendo; it is the quiet music of a life well-lived – in everyday moments, small delights, simple joys.

When we view happiness as a 'goal', we distance ourselves from it. Instead of striving for a specific point of happiness, what if we shift the focus to finding joy in everyday moments, the journey itself? The perspective emphasizes living in the present, enjoying activities that bring joy.

Emotional intelligence invites us to be mindful, to live fully in the present. This is how we encounter happiness often, rather than chase it endlessly.

We seem to be only talking of happiness this far.

How does sorrow fit into the whole thing?

If meeting expectations brings joy; not meeting them will make us sad. Right?

Right.

To pursue happiness is to take risk that you may not find it. To be happy is a risk that in future you may not be.

Sadness, like any other emotion, needs to be accepted first. If we do not accept sorrow, it stays with us as 'anger'.

Why anger? Because anger is our defence mechanism that offers the illusion of control. For example, someone who loses a job may express grief as rage toward the employer. This is not uncommon.

Happiness is a comparative emotion. Its sweetness is understood in contrast to suffering. After a slip disc injury last year, just walking a few steps pain-free filled me with immense joy.

To truly feel happiness therefore, we must have experienced sorrow – they are **Siamese twins**, inseparable.

We tend to assume happiness is a straight line, but it's not. It moves more like a wave on something wild – up and down, erratic, unpredictable – and yet still real, still ours. We can take control of our happiness, regulating it via our goals, expectations and our attitude.

Pervasive happiness. Found in the quiet joy of being understood, reconnecting with childhood memory when hearing an old song, watching someone you nurtured succeed...

So, even amidst grief, hope can linger around and hum softly in our ears - *tomorrow is another day!*

Chapter 9: Selfishness, Misunderstood Virtue

Happiness and fear - both are deeply tied to one idea: **selfishness**

A crude definition of selfish person is, "*someone who thinks of own happiness before others*".

Fear is also for oneself, for one's loved ones and for one's possessions. Does the instinct to protect them reveal selfishness? And if so, doesn't that make everyone selfish?

Why is it, then, that we all act selfishly, yet recoil at being called selfish?

I believe it is because, we misunderstand 'selfishness'- not for what it truly is, but for how it appears. Much like we often misjudge anger, we mislabel selfishness as something shameful, rather than something human.

Let us dispel our misconceptions.

One cannot give what one does not have. I cannot bring joy to others if I am unhappy. By nourishing my own well-being, I become more capable of uplifting those around me. [NG1] If seeking my own happiness is considered selfish, then this selfishness serves others too.

Consider airplane safety instructions: *"Put on your oxygen mask before helping others."* In essence, take care of yourself so you're able to take care of others.

Yet we often celebrate those who neglect themselves for others – tirelessly giving while ignoring their own needs. These individuals are hailed as selfless, even saintly.

But are they, truly?

I understand – this is a difficult question to confront. It cuts into a core belief many of us have been conditioned to hold: that charity, goodness, and virtue begin with the act of giving ourselves away. That martyrdom is moral. That self-sacrifice is the highest form of love.

Yet, what if this belief, noble as it is, is simply incomplete?

As a mother, I've come to realize something surprising: when I put my child's needs before my own, it's not always an act of selflessness – it's often deeply personal, even selfish.

Why?

Because it brings *me* joy.

Because my well-being is intertwined with my child's. If they struggle, I can't help but step in – not only out of love, but because their success validates something within me. It reassures me that I am a good parent in the eyes of others, and perhaps more importantly, in my own eyes. If my child thrives, I feel fulfilled. If they falter, I feel anxious, even inadequate. Therefore, in helping them, I'm also protecting myself from sadness, from the ache of feeling like I've failed.

If we are brutally honest and truly objective, we will notice this uncomfortable phenomenon: when we wish or pray for someone's well-being, it is often because their suffering weighs on *us* too. Their pain becomes our burden – emotionally, mentally, even spiritually. In that sense, our desire for their welfare is a selfish desire; it is tied to our own longing for relief, peace, or emotional harmony.

Even science agrees: acts of kindness release dopamine, oxytocin, and endorphins – chemicals that make *you* feel happy. When you make someone smile, you're not just giving; you're also receiving a chemical reward. It *feels good to do good* – and we often seek that feeling. Helping others, then, isn't purely altruistic – it's also an act of emotional self-nourishment.

So being selfish is not that bad. Many of our so-called selfless acts are subtly tied to a personal need –

- It provides validation, to feel like a good mother, daughter, spouse or friend
- It makes *you* feel good.
- It improves *your* self-image.
- It strengthens *your* relationships.
- It gives *you* meaning.

The truth is, we ultimately do what we *want* to do. Psychologists have long observed that when faced with choices, we tend to select the one that brings us the most satisfaction – even if it doesn't look that way on the surface. Take, for example, those who unconsciously cast themselves in the role of the victim. While it may appear disempowering, there can be a hidden reward – attention, sympathy, or a sense of significance.

In short, being selfish is perhaps our natural way to exist.

After observing many people who take pride in sacrifice – and having spent time myself trying to make choices solely for the sake of others – I've come to believe that selfishness is a deeply misunderstood virtue.

To make someone else happy, there must be, at some level, a desire within *me* to see them happy. That internal alignment is what sustains the act. Without it, the façade eventually cracks. Resentment creeps in. I start to feel used, depleted, even betrayed.

If I don't find joy in caring for my child, I may begin to resent the role – and unfairly, the child. This applies to every role we play: parent, partner, friend, employee. *Sacrifice without choice* is not sustainable. *Sacrifice by choice*, never feels like a sacrifice.

Choice. That's the key word.

We must learn to choose what truly makes us happy – not just what brings momentary relief.

Happiness is different from pleasure.

Pleasure is often impulsive. It offers a fleeting escape – a sugar rush for the soul. Like the ice cream that delights our sweet tooth but derails our health goals. Or that quick fix of social approval – a like, a compliment, a title – that eventually gives way to emptiness or backlash.

Sometimes, pleasure masquerades as peace. We avoid conflict, postpone hard conversations, or ignore uncomfortable truths – not because it serves us in the long run, but because it spares us short-term pain. Like skipping an injection, only to end up needing surgery.

Happiness, on the other hand, is deeper.

It is the compass guiding every human action – a movement away from pain and toward love, comfort, and safety.

Whatever threatens our happiness, it evokes fear. Fear, when unexamined, often transforms into anger. We start to hate the source of threat.

To break this cycle, we must reclaim ownership of our happiness. That means being *wisely selfish* – guarding our joy not with entitlement, but with responsibility. True happiness cannot be outsourced. No one else can create it for us. Only we can.

True happiness spills over. A truly happy person is often kind, patient, generous, and resilient. For example, a teacher who finds joy in their vocation not only feels fulfilled but also inspires and uplifts students. In contrast, a person chasing only pleasure (e.g., wealth, attention, thrill) may become more self-centred and less sensitive to others' needs.

Here's the real distinction:

The problem isn't *selfishness*. It's **greed**.

Greed is ***self-centred***. There is a distinction. Being self-centric is an over-preoccupation with one's own needs, fears, and imagined deprivations. This is self-serving behaviour that may harm, ignore, or even exploit others.

Greed emerges not from self-love, but from fear – the fear that someone else holds the key to your joy. That they may deny it, take it, or give it selectively. That fear drives us to snatch, to hoard, to dominate.

But when I reclaim the truth – that only *I* can increase or decrease my happiness – my selfishness becomes *benevolent.* I stop stealing joy. I start radiating it.

Yes, I am selfish. And I say it without guilt. Because I'm no longer in denial.

I am awake – and accountable – to my own joy.

Chapter 10: Obligation, Ultimate Motivator

Motivation – quite literally, a stimulus that moves us. It drives us forward in pursuit of a goal, typically with the expectation of a reward.

Broadly, motivation is classified into:

- **Intrinsic Motivation** - Doing something because we *want* to. Driven by internal satisfaction – the joy of the activity itself. Examples include curiosity, personal challenge, or simply having fun.

- **Extrinsic Motivation** - Doing something because we *need* to. Driven by external rewards – money, grades, status, or security.

An extreme hypothetical example of intrinsically motivated person will be: Smita works not because she has to, but because she *loves* what she does. She's financially secure, owns her home, and wants for nothing. Yet she continues to work because it brings her meaning and joy.

An extreme hypothetical example of extrinsically motivated person will be: Anna works solely to pay her bills and support her family. Her job brings her no fulfilment, no opportunities for growth. But she must carry on.

Most of us exist somewhere in the middle – we work to earn a living but also find satisfaction in the work itself or in the relationships it fosters. There's usually some blend of internal and external reward.

But what happens when a task offers *neither* intrinsic pleasure *nor* extrinsic benefit?

Logically, we might avoid it. But we don't – not always. And we all know this.

Why do we still show up for certain tasks, conversations, or commitments?

Because of something deeper – **obligation**.

Obligation arises from our internal code of ethics – our personal sense of right and wrong, shaped by our values. It compels us to act, not for reward, but because it feels inherently right. In this way, obligation becomes one of the most powerful forms of motivation – quiet, persistent, and enduring.

In goal-setting sessions, people are often advised to *publicly* declare their goals – to a trusted few. Why? Because this creates a sense of obligation. Now, there's a promise to uphold. And with it, a deeper commitment.

As a personal coach, I also engage with parents. A recurring pain point emerges: *"My children don't care for me the way I cared for them."* I've reflected on this – and on my own relationship with my parents.

I, too, found myself expecting more from them than they expected of me. I wanted them to always behave, understand, be composed – essentially, to "know better." When they didn't, I'd grow irritated. Then guilt would follow. I'd try to correct myself. But the change wouldn't last. And the cycle repeated.

Why? Why wasn't I motivated enough to consistently treat my parents with the compassion they deserved – even though I genuinely cared for them?

The answer revealed something profound: *Obligation is the ultimate motivator often more powerful than intrinsic or extrinsic rewards.*

Why Parents Feel More Obligated

Parents often feel a stronger sense of duty toward their children than children do toward them. Why?

- Because the child exists as a result of their decision – a life they chose to bring into the world. That choice brings responsibility.

- Because parents often invest their hopes and dreams in their children – a kind of emotional legacy they feel compelled to nurture.

- Because society expects perfection from parents – reflected in the behaviour of their children.

Children, on the other hand, bear none of this. They didn't choose their parents. They're not living through them. Aside from a biological bond and some social expectations, there's little that *automatically* obliges them to care.

That's why, especially in adolescence – when rebellion against social norms peaks – parental disappointment often deepens.

Some children, of course, are naturally more empathetic. They *enjoy* caring. It is an intrinsic reward for them. For some others, loyalty and sense of duty towards parents, is seeded early – often through cultural conditioning. From that sense of duty grows a natural inclination to act with empathy – it feels like the only way to honour the bonds they hold sacred. Essentially, sense of duty brings sense of obligation.

Unquestioned loyalty, like superstition, can lead to fanaticism – even war. Any belief adopted without critical thinking becomes brittle, easily manipulated, and potentially harmful. True loyalty, like true care, must come from *choice*.

It's easy to stay committed to beliefs we've chosen for ourselves. Those imposed upon us often feel restrictive – and with restriction comes the temptation to break free.

The healthiest parent-child relationships are rooted not in obligation alone, but in mutual respect and affection – where questions are welcome, not silenced. Open communication leads to understanding and mutual empathy. In such relationships, care becomes *voluntary. Chosen.* And in that choosing, it transforms from duty to *intrinsic* motivation.

Obligation as a Conscious Tool

When I recognize the power of obligation, I can *consciously* use it to my advantage. I can attach a sense of duty to meaningful goals – whether professional, relational, or personal. As a child, I can reflect: *Why should I care for my parents?* Not because I'm told to, but because I *choose* to understand their journey, their humanity, their aging.

Obligation can also be directed inward – to *self*. It becomes a shield against exploitation and regret.

I learned this the painful way – after losing my father.

In his final days, he suffered deeply. Witnessing that suffering was excruciating. I was haunted by memories of my impatience, my cold words, my urging him to "fix" his anxieties – as if it were that easy for a man who had survived two brain strokes. I was 40 then. Old enough to know better.

There was no way I could go back in time and be nicer to him. But I *did* want to be nice to him. I *did* love him. So why had I lost control sometimes?

Because I was afraid.

Afraid to acknowledge that the man I leaned on – the source of my values – was fading. Losing his edge. No longer invincible.

It's terrifying to watch strength decay in the people we've always depended on.

But that fear, once acknowledged, released me from guilt. It ushered in *awareness* – a clearer understanding of what was truly driving behaviour and feelings.

Out of awareness emerges a motivation rooted in values, not shame. Eventually, this value-led motivation evolves into a deep, chosen sense of obligation – not imposed from outside, but accepted from within.

Obligation is a potent force – one of the most underrated motivators in human behaviour. But it must be *conscious*. It must be *examined*. When rooted in self-awareness, obligation can drive growth, deepen relationships, and elevate purpose.

I can now choose to feel obligated to be efficient, accountable, and compassionate —as a professional, as a citizen, and as a human being.

And just as importantly, when my obligations bring only pain or keep me bound to unhealthy dynamics, I can release them – freeing myself from relationships or roles that exploit rather than empower. After all, the first and foremost obligation we owe – is to *ourselves.*

Chapter 11: Values, My Personal Treasure

The magic of Emotional Intelligence (EI) is such that once you begin the journey, each insight becomes a stepping stone to another – and the view keeps getting more rewarding.

During times of introspection, when I started thinking deeply about my goals, I discovered something crucial: goals are only truly attainable when they align with our *values*. If a goal requires me to compromise on something I deeply value, no matter how shiny or appealing it looks on the surface, I'll eventually feel resistance. Motivation will erode, and I'll likely quit.

I saw this play out all around me. People often blame themselves – labelling themselves as lazy, weak-willed, or inconsistent – when in fact, the real issue is misalignment between their goals and their values.

Take this simple example: I set a fitness goal that requires me to wake up early and exercise. But I stay up late because the only time I get to enjoy my family is after work, when we're all finally home. Eventually, I start missing workouts. Not because I don't *want* to be fit – but because, unconsciously, I'm choosing something I value more: time with my loved ones.

If I then label myself lazy or undisciplined, I not only abandon the goal, I damage my self-image. That inner frustration may even spill out in hurtful ways – blaming my family for my lack of progress, for instance.

But if I pause and reflect, I realize this isn't a failure – it's a *natural prioritization*. I'm making a conscious choice to honour something I care about. That awareness softens my inner critic. It also opens a door: I can now ask, *how do I design a goal that supports my values, instead of opposing them?*

The Essential Link Between Goals and Values

Before setting meaningful goals, I must first understand not only my desires, passions, and talents – but also my *values*. These are the non-negotiables, the aspects of life I refuse to compromisc on.

Consider this: someone may have a God-given talent for singing and a deep passion for it. But if they value privacy above all else, then a career in playback singing – with its public scrutiny might slowly eat away at them. Or a brilliant salesperson with dreams of becoming head of marketing might find that constant travel pulls them away from family – a value they hold sacred. Even if they reach the title, they may find it hollow.

In short, we can *succeed* without being *happy*. But when our goals are grounded in our values, success becomes sustainable, meaningful and *joyful*.

If I had to distil this into a formula:

Talent + Passion = Success

But,

Talent + Passion + *Values* = Happiness

And ultimately, isn't *happiness* the goal behind every other goal?

Values Vs Core Values

A value is something you believe is important. Values guide your behaviour, but not all of them have the same weight.

Examples: You might value *efficiency*, *health*, or *teamwork* – these are important, but they might shift depending on your role, environment, or goals. They are often contextual. You might prioritize *ambition* at work, but *playfulness* at home.

A **core value** is non-negotiable. It's a fundamental part of who you are – so deeply embedded that violating it feels like betraying yourself. They rarely change, even as you grow or face different life stages. When you're living *against* a core value, you often feel stressed, lost, or inauthentic.

Imagine someone who values *success* and *integrity*. If success is just a value, they might compromise a little to achieve a goal.

But if integrity is a *core value*, they'll refuse to lie or manipulate – even if it costs them success.

A core value is something you will not negotiate with life, no matter the cost.

Finding your *core* personal values is essential because they are the foundation of a meaningful, coherent, and self-directed life. Bedrock of your identity.

When I ask people about their core values during goal-setting sessions, one answer frequently emerges: *honesty*. They may use different words – truth, integrity – but the essence remains the same.

Yet if honesty is such a universally held core value, why is dishonesty so prevalent?

Because what most people value is *others* being honest with them. It's an expectation – not a core value they consistently uphold within themselves.

Similarly, someone may say they value money. But money, in itself, isn't the value. What they may truly value is *comfort, freedom*, or *status*. Money is just the means.

Discovering Core Values

You can value many things, but you can only have a few core values.

Life is one core value – something most of us wouldn't trade for anything. Beyond that, the question that helped me identify my core values was:

- *What would I refuse to compromise on, unless my life depended on it?*

Other reflective prompts:

- What consistently makes me angry or frustrated? (Anger is emerging from fear – and fear reveals what we deeply care about.)
- What brings me deep joy?

After rounds of introspection, I arrived at a small set of 3-4 *core values* – the true treasures I cannot comfortably sacrifice. When these are threatened, I become defensive. When I do compromise on them, the discomfort is so intense it becomes unsustainable.

Conversely, when I know these values are protected, I gain the capacity to engage even in less enjoyable tasks. For example, if my husband can carve out an hour in the morning to play on the beach – honouring his love for the outdoors – he finds the next eight hours at his laptop more bearable.

That's the power of nurturing our core values: they act as inner fuel.

Designing Aligned Goals

Armed with clarity about what I value most, I can design goals that don't create inner conflict – goals I'm *truly* motivated to achieve. With this alignment, I no longer sabotage my progress or mislabel myself as a failure.

Instead, I move forward with both energy and ease – because now, my goals aren't battling my values; they are being *carried* by them.

Chapter 12: From Awareness to Control

It's life. It doesn't bend to my command.

Even on a day that comes close to my ideal, there's almost always that *one* thing that doesn't quite go as I imagined. And let's be honest – most days aren't anywhere near perfect.

But here's what I've learned: the more I pause to tune into my emotions, to respond with awareness rather than react on impulse, the more I feel empowered to *shape* my day – even if I can't control every detail. That sense of inner control brings satisfaction. Positivity builds naturally, and I pass it on. People respond to that energy, and their warmth amplifies mine. Suddenly, everything doesn't *need* to be perfect.

Even a dream job comes with some less-than-enjoyable tasks. But the joy of doing something I love every day helps me carry the weight of what I don't. Doing even a *few* things my way – with intention and joy – makes the rest manageable.

That one small pause for self-awareness changed everything. It gave me the power to regulate my emotions, thoughts, responses, and choices. And because I'm choosing consciously, I experience less regret. There's less blame, less shame.

I know I acted the way I did because, in that moment, after reflection, it felt like the best decision. I did my best. That's all any human can do. I can't predict the future. I don't know how my choices will intersect with others or what consequences will unfold. But I do know this: no matter what happens, I can always pause, reflect, and choose again – with a little more wisdom each time.

So yes, I have no one to blame. But equally powerful – I have no one to *wait* for. I hold the skill to carve my life with my own hands.

And once I gained that control over myself, I began to *see* others more clearly. Not as people to be fixed, but as individuals navigating their own inner world.

Because here's the truth I've come to trust –

No number of instructions can push the 'self'. 'Self' does that when 'self' is somehow 'self'-convinced that it is in best 'self'-interest!

No amount of advice, preaching, or persuasion can change someone unless *they* are convinced that change serves their best interest. Only the *self* can control the self.

Transformation is thus an inside job. I can't change others – only they can, when they're ready, when *they* believe it serves them.

What *can* I do?

I can live my truth. I can strive for my personal excellence – and perhaps, just perhaps, my authenticity will inspire someone to begin their own journey.

Personal excellence inspires **social excellence.**

SOCIAL EXCELLENCE

Chapter 13: Control Vs Manage, The Vital Shift

All future learning arises from comparisons with patterns we've previously stored in memory. It's like recognizing a new flower—say, a lily. To identify it, we subconsciously compare it with flowers we already know, like a rose or a lotus. When we realize it's neither, we add the lily to our internal library of flower patterns.

The same principle applies to human behaviour. The more people we meet, the more behavioural patterns we observe. As we witness their emotional journeys and motivations, we grow more capable of interpreting and responding to these patterns effectively.

Understanding Others Starts Within

In truth, we understand others *through* ourselves. That's why we more easily relate to those who resemble us. If I have a fear of lizards, I can empathize with someone who shares that fear. If I don't, I may dismiss their fear as irrational.

"*Do unto others as you would have them do unto you.*" The Golden Rule. I grew up hearing this, as many of us did. But looking closer—it presupposes self-awareness. For example, I've noticed how much I dislike being told to "calm down" or having my anger questioned. That awareness now shapes how I treat others when they are angry.

Yet, the true pinnacle of self-awareness is realizing that each of us is fundamentally unique. Even identical twins are shaped by unique blend of nature and nurture. Nature factors, which include our genes and our physical features and Nurture factors, which include our environment and life experiences.

We have explored the power of beliefs to shape our reality; now, let us turn to the deeper question: how are these beliefs formed in the first place?

In my live sessions, I use playful exercises to illustrate how easily our minds can be conditioned. Try this one quickly and honestly:

- Say aloud "SILK" five times.
- Now spell "SILK."
- Say it one more time.

Q: What do cows drink?

If you answered "milk," you're not alone. The correct answer is water—but your brain likely defaulted to the associated sound pattern.

Such exercises highlight how swiftly the human brain forms and repeats patterns. In matter of seconds - even when they override what we logically know to be true.

Now imagine how deeply conditioned our minds become over the years. Everything we have heard or even overheard, read, seen in real life or on TV/films, all communication we have ever had with our parents, teachers, neighbours, colleagues, friends...even strangers. Every message that has been received by our brain directly or indirectly must have conditioned it. Any message that was repeated, the conditioning reaffirmed.

If just a few seconds of conditioning can so clearly influence our responses, imagine the impact of a lifetime of repeated messages and experiences. This cumulative conditioning shapes our belief system.

Consider the famous "Five Monkeys" experiment:

Five monkeys are placed in a cage. A banana hangs above a ladder. One monkey climbs the ladder to get the banana—and all the monkeys are doused with cold water. This happens a few times. Eventually, none of the monkeys dare climb the ladder. One by one, each original monkey is replaced. The new monkeys, unaware of the cold water, are still beaten down by the others if they attempt to climb. Eventually, none of the monkeys in the cage have ever been sprayed, yet none attempt to take the banana. The behaviour persists—because the belief persists.

Many of our beliefs work the same way: they're passed down, rarely tested, and sometimes maintained without understanding their origins. Some beliefs are difficult or impossible to test—like "Everything happens for a reason".

Often, when we cannot test our beliefs, we pass them on to others—especially our children—convincing or even pressuring them to adopt the same views. In doing so, we're not just teaching; we're seeking reassurance. The more people who share our beliefs, the more validated we feel. After all, our conditioning tells us there's safety in numbers—what the majority thinks must be right. However, since our actions stem from our beliefs, this unexamined transmission doesn't just limit our potential (our 'bananas,' so to speak); it also poses a deeper risk - the risk of living someone else's life without realizing it.

If all our new learning happens in light of past patterns, they are important. The issue isn't that our minds form patterns—This, in fact, protects us from potential harm. Issue is that we start to think our patterns are the only valid ones. That's when we stop looking, stop learning, and begin rejecting anything (or anyone) that doesn't fit what we know. It's ironic—we all seek to be unique yet often reject the uniqueness in others.

I like being myself, and you take pride in who you are—so why would either of us readily adopt the other's patterns? We wouldn't. That's why true change cannot be imposed; it must come from within. You cannot change me unless I choose to change. And I will only make that choice when I feel genuinely inspired or believe that the change will serve me. The same holds true for everyone.

The only person we can truly control is ourselves. Others, we can only ***manage***—through understanding. When we understand someone's beliefs and values, we uncover the reasons behind their behaviour. *Then*, we may influence them by our own behaviour and actions.

Chapter 14: Expansion, The Remaining Two Pillers

Emotional intelligence serves as the foundation for personal excellence as well as social excellence. Personal excellence is a powerful driver of social skill development however it does not guarantee social excellence.

Self-awareness helps understanding others but doesn't automatically lead to it. Here are a few key reasons why the link isn't automatic:

1. **Self-absorption vs. self-awareness**: Self-awareness can sometimes veer into self-absorption. A person might become so focused on their own experiences, emotions, or wounds that they struggle to see beyond them or assume others feel the same way.

2. **Judgment remains**: Even with self-awareness, we may continue to judge emotions—ours or others—as valid or invalid. True connection requires not just recognizing feelings but suspending judgment to understand them as they are. Shift from 'right or wrong' to 'what and why - the curiosity reframes the moment not as a verdict, but as a doorway to understanding.

3. **Unprocessed pain**: Awareness of one's own emotions doesn't guarantee healing. If we haven't processed our pain, we may project it onto others or react defensively rather than with understanding.

If self-awareness and self-control are the pillars of personal excellence, the pillars for social excellence are **Empathy and Effective Communication**.

Just as self-awareness leads to self-control, empathy deepens your relational intelligence, making communication effective.

Empathy is not easy, but when developed, it becomes a bridge to deep human connection—making communication not only accurate, but truly meaningful. Empathy grows through deliberate openness, curiosity, and humility toward others' inner lives, naturally fostering authentic and effective interaction. Genuine communication is rooted in mutual understanding.

At the heart of quality communication is active listening – the willingness to understand before trying to be understood, which makes it an act of empathy.

Listening signals, "You matter. I'm here to understand you." This shift in focus transforms communication from a struggle for dominance into a shared effort toward connection. When practiced fully, it turns conflict from a battleground into a space for collaborative, win-win solutions. More often than not, conflict doesn't stem from unbridgeable differences, but from the rigid boundaries of our own perceptions.

Chapter 15: Empathy, The Invisible Bridge

Empathy is the ability to feel what another person feels. It goes deeper than sympathy, which is about caring and understanding from the outside. Empathy, in contrast, invites us to step into someone else's shoes and see the world through their eyes.

True empathy demands the suspension of your own beliefs, truths, and perceptions. It asks you to temporarily adopt someone else's reality without judgment. When you manage to do that, even for a fleeting moment, you experience what could be called a moment of pure empathy. It's not just understanding someone—it's becoming them, emotionally and cognitively, for that brief connection. You feel what they feel, with the same emotional intensity, shaped by the same internal logic.

It is difficult—perhaps even elusive—but not unattainable.

The Brain's Role in Empathy

Our capacity for empathy is not just a personality trait—it is deeply rooted in our neurobiology. The brain is wired for connection. Specific neural networks, such as the mirror neuron system, allow us to simulate and internally mirror the emotions of others. When we observe someone in pain or joy, similar regions in our own brain light up as if we were experiencing it ourselves. This neurological mirroring is the foundation of **emotional empathy**.

At the same time, the prefrontal cortex—the brain's centre for rational thinking and self-regulation—helps us engage in **cognitive empathy**, allowing us to take another person's perspective while managing our own emotions. But this balance is delicate. Under stress or emotional overload, the brain shifts into survival mode, often reducing the capacity for empathy. This is why we can find it harder to empathize when we are angry, anxious, or overwhelmed. Our emotional brain hijacks our thinking brain.

Yet the opposite is also true: the brain can change—and so can our capacity for empathy. This is the promise of neuroplasticity. When we consciously practice empathy, we strengthen the neural pathways that support it. Over time, with intention and repetition, we can become more emotionally attuned and more capable of stepping into someone else's inner world.

How the Brain Changes with Age

Empathy, like many brain functions, evolves over time. As we age, our brains undergo both structural and functional changes. While certain types of processing speed and memory may decline, research shows that emotional intelligence and empathic understanding often increase with age.

When we are younger, our brains are still developing the structures needed for deep perspective-taking and emotional regulation. Children and even young adults may struggle to fully grasp the emotional world of their parents, often interpreting their actions through a self-centred lens: *Why are they so strict? Why don't they understand me? Why can't they be more like other parents?*

Children, across generations, face fewer expectations to be perfect, while parents often feel pressured to meet unrealistic standards. Add to it: In past generations, family roles were more clearly defined, and children were expected to defer to parental authority. Today, there's a stronger focus on children's emotional well-being and autonomy, which can sometimes overshadow the importance of teaching them reciprocal responsibility.

Thus, children may feel little obligation to treat their parents in a particular way, yet they often expect their parents to meet specific emotional or material needs. This imbalance – entitlement without responsibility – erodes empathy.

But as we grow older—and our brains develop greater emotional depth—our understanding expands. We are likely to begin to see not just *what* our parents did, but *why*; Start to appreciate their sacrifices, their fears, and the invisible weight they carried. With this shift, empathy emerges—not just for who they were as "parents," but for who they are as people. We move from critique to care. From rebellion to respect. And that shift, perhaps more than anything, defines emotional adulthood.

This is why it's not uncommon for adult children to say, *"I didn't understand my parents until I became one,"* or *"Now I see what they were going through."* These are not just reflections of life experience—they are signs of a brain that has matured emotionally, and that now has the capacity to hold complexity, contradiction, and compassion at once.

Age often brings perspective. Life experience deepens our understanding of human struggle, loss, joy, and complexity. This richer emotional tapestry enhances our ability to relate, not just from the head, but from the heart. That's why many people find that empathy becomes more instinctive with maturity—not because the world gets simpler, but because we've learned to carry more of it within ourselves.

Yet empathy is not guaranteed to grow endlessly with age. In old age, empathy can sometimes wane again—not out of selfishness, but from weariness. Physical decline, chronic pain, loneliness, or cognitive changes can narrow emotional bandwidth. When life becomes a battle for one's own stability and comfort, it becomes harder to carry the emotional weight of others. The mind, once expansive in understanding others, may turn inward again—this time from exhaustion rather than immaturity.

So, the arc of empathy is not linear. It can expand, contract, and be reshaped by circumstance. The challenge—and the opportunity—is to recognize these shifts in ourselves and in those around us. To meet entitlement in youth with patience, to meet aging with compassion, and to hold empathy as a living, breathing practice—one that requires continual tending, at every stage of life.

Seeing Ourselves Through Others' Eyes

To empathize truly, we must also be able to view ourselves objectively—as others see us. This is challenging because we tend to evaluate ourselves based on our own beliefs. Take, for example, the role of a spouse. We often act according to our personal definition of a "good" partner, expecting our efforts to be recognized and appreciated. So, it can come as a surprise—even a shock—when our spouse sees us differently.

At such moments, we instinctively defend ourselves. We justify our actions, convinced we've been "right." And in that defensiveness, empathy vanishes.

Consider this familiar scenario:

A wife complains, "He runs our home like it's his office. He's responsible and caring, yes – but always prioritizes tasks over people."

The husband, confused, replies, "I've been a good husband. I've worked hard, never cheated, never done anything illegal or immoral. Why are you unhappy?"

She responds, "You are all those things. But you don't give me what I need – you don't *listen.* You don't even try to understand."

Throughout their marriage, he played the role of the "good husband" – but only by *his* definition. The truth? A person is only a good spouse if *their partner* feels they are. Because it's the partner who gives meaning to that role.

This principle holds true for every relationship – parent-child, employer-employee, friend-friend. We are only as effective in a role as the other person *experiences* us to be. And understanding this is the heart of empathy.

When empathizing, we try to imagine the situations from other person's perspective rather than ours. We momentarily suspend our own perspective and inhabit someone else's reality. This requires vulnerability – the courage to put aside our convictions and open ourselves to another truth.

Empathy is something we often expect from others but struggle to offer ourselves. It is a choice, and a difficult one –

because we're deeply attached to our own belief of right and wrong. Empathy means confronting the possibility that our truth may not be *the* truth.

Through my own journey of personal growth, I've come to understand that our sense of right and wrong – our "reality" – is shaped by our conditioning. *Had I lived someone else's life, I might have believed exactly what they believe, felt what they feel.*

To empathize deeply, I must see from *their* eyes. For a moment, I must adopt their beliefs – without judgment, without resistance. And when I do, I often find myself thinking, *Of course. Now I understand.*

Empathy, when practiced, can transform not just relationships, but results. Let me share an example.

While working as an IT delivery manager, I approached a long-time client for a software contract renewal. To my surprise, he expressed frustration with our technical team and dissatisfaction with the product – saying he was unlikely to renew.

My first impulse was to defend our work - but I paused. Instead, I said, "I'm sure you have valid reasons to feel this way. If switching the product is best for your business, I will help make the transition smooth."

As he shared his perspective, I listened without judgment, placing myself in his shoes. In doing so, I not only understood his frustrations, but also saw clearly where we needed to improve.

Once I had truly listened, I responded with honesty –

acknowledging the gaps, clarifying our policies, and outlining the costs and risks of switching. That moment shifted everything. Feeling heard and supported, he chose to renew – and even funded product enhancements. It became a true win-win.

Empathy allowed me to influence without manipulation – no false promises, no sales tactics. Just understanding.

One may still wonder if trying to always understand the other person may not put a burden on one. When the empathy is in expectation of instant reciprocation, it may. However, in long run, it is more rewarding than draining. It is liberating and fulfilling.

The truth is, most people are simply looking for someone who gets them – their fears, their frustrations, their dreams. When they feel understood, they become willing to understand in return.

It's often just a matter of *who goes first*.

An emotionally intelligent person doesn't let ego block connection. They're willing to take that first step – and in doing so, they begin a virtuous cycle.

Of course, being empathetic is not equivalent to being exploited. If the other person refuses to hold an empathetic hand, the hand can be withdrawn after a reasonable wait. *After all, that is also empathy - to understand that the other person does not want to be understood, at least at present or, by us.* Others' reaction is the reflection of their needs, not our ability.

How do we build empathy

When listening, try to identify and reflect the other person's emotion. Say, "When that happened, you must have felt... right?" If they agree, you've connected. If not, they'll correct you – and you'll learn how they *really* feel.

When the other person is sharing how they feel, instead of asking "Is this a valid emotion?", ask:

"What is this feeling trying to say?"

"Why might this person (or I) be feeling this way?"

This curiosity softens judgment. We don't have to become blank slates free of judgment. We just have to be *bigger* than our judgment. We have to notice it, hold it gently, and choose not to let it close the door on connection.

This practise deepens our emotional intelligence. It teaches us about different personalities, value systems, and worldviews – all of which make us better listeners, better leaders, and ultimately, better humans.

Empathy makes us better communicators. Diplomacy is not about persuasion. It's about resonance and empathy is the key to unlocking it. When we anticipate others' needs and motivations, we learn to speak in a way that resonates. Once we understand *why* someone feels or acts a certain way, we can meet them where they are – and gently guide them toward where they need to go. Empathy, the invisible bridge, helps us connect and then influence.

Chapter 16:
Listening, The Empathy Tool

At first glance, listening might seem like a simple act of hearing words. But true listening goes far beyond that – it is an act of empathy in motion.

The next time someone opens up to you, try to really listen. Set aside the urge to advise, to compare, to interrupt. That person isn't just sharing their problem; they're reaching out for understanding. Full acknowledgment is the first act of care.

Here's a metaphor to reflect on: *If a glass falls in an empty room, does it make a sound?* Science says – it creates sound waves but for there to be **sound**, there must be an **ear** to receive it.

Without someone to receive the message, speaking loses its power. Listening is not just half of communication – it is its soul.

We all talk to be understood. Yet we often listen only to respond – to opine, to advise, to judge, to redirect. This is because we mistakenly view listening as a passive act, and feel that unless we *talk*, we aren't really participating.

Real listening is anything but passive. It is an active, intentional engagement. We must resist the reflex to take our turn and instead, give our full presence.

Let's take a simple, hypothetical example.

Spouse comes home after a long day and begins to share: "*Work is exhausting. Deadlines are crushing. My boss just doesn't get it.*"

Here are some common responses:

1. **"You need a break. Just take some time off."**

   → *Advice.* Sounds logical, but it misses the point. Spouse may feel dismissed – "If it were that simple, I'd have done it. Anyway he/she wouldn't understand. Let me just stop talking about it or it will lead to an argument"

2. **"You always let people walk over you."**

   → *Judgment.* Now the spouse feels blamed. The conversation shuts down.

3. **"You think that's bad? My day was worse..."**

→ *Comparison.* Empathy becomes a contest – and no one wins.

4. **"Let's forget it. Want to watch a movie?"**

→ *Diversion.* The issue is brushed away. End of Conversation!

In all these cases, the conversation didn't end because no one spoke. It ended because no one *listened.*

We do not fail to listen out of malice – we simply haven't been taught how. Look at how we educate our children:

Over twelve years are dedicated to reading and writing. Yet listening – which accounts for nearly **45%** of all communication – receives no formal training.

We also need to challenge the idea that listening is "passive activity". The phrase "passive activity" is a contradiction in first place. An oxymoron.

Professor Albert Mehrabian, a pioneer in human communication research, demonstrated that only **7%** of meaning in a message is conveyed through words. **38%** comes through tone of voice, and **55%** through body language.

Consider this example:

Verbal: "I don't have a problem with you."

Non-verbal: Avoids eye contact, arms crossed, voice tight with tension.

Which message do you trust? The words – or the body?

Hearing takes ears – but listening? If 93% of communication happens beyond words, then listening goes far beyond sound.

Listening isn't just about hearing – it's about *receiving*. We listen with our eyes, our posture, our intuition. We ask open-ended questions. We attune not only to what is said, but also to what's left unsaid.

As we move through life, accumulating experiences and a deeper understanding of the world, our *potential* to listen more effectively naturally increases. However, whether we *actually* harness this potential depends on several factors – our personality, the context, and critically, whether we've managed to unlearn the bad habits we've picked up along the way.

Listening, like any frequently used skill, is easy to take for granted and to perform poorly without realizing it. Consider driving: we're initially trained to follow certain best practices – check mirrors, signal appropriately, keep both hands on the wheel in the "10 and 2" position. But as we grow confident, we often become lax. We rely on autopilot. What was once conscious discipline gives way to convenience. Listening follows a similar arc. Over time, we may lose the precision and presence that good listening requires, replacing it with assumptions, impatience, or habitual distraction.

It's important to note that effective listening has little correlation with traditional intelligence. High IQ or a strong vocabulary might help us process information more quickly, but they don't automatically make us better listeners. In fact, highly intelligent individuals may be *more* prone to mental drift – bored by familiar conversations or too quick to predict what's being said, they tune out before truly hearing.

True listening requires more than intellect. It requires humility, discipline, and the willingness to stay fully present – even when we think we already know.

Here's what makes listening even harder:

Our brains process speech at 125-250 words per minute. But we think at 1000-3000 words per minute. That leaves a lot of spare mental bandwidth – which often gets hijacked by mental chatter. Instead of staying with the speaker, we drift. We plan responses, recall unrelated memories, or judge what's being said. Effective listening requires us to silence that chatter.

Now imagine how that earlier spouse conversation might change with real listening:

Spouse: *"Work is exhausting. Boss is impossible."*

Partner:

- *"You really do look tired."*
- *"Is it the workload – or something else?"*
- *"Is your boss not supportive?"*
- *"Is this just a rough patch, or something deeper?"*
- *"Are you still enjoying your job?"*

See the difference?

It begins with a simple reflection – "You look tired" – which immediately validates the speaker's emotion. From there, thoughtful questions follow.

Through gentle, open-ended questions, the listener helps the speaker unpack their own truth. Maybe the frustration is about the job. Or the boss. Or just one overwhelming day. But now, the speaker has a partner in that discovery.

That is the beauty of empathetic listening. You don't offer solutions – you help the other person *find* theirs.

Being heard – truly heard – is a powerful experience. It makes us feel seen, valued, understood. In contrast, unsolicited advice often makes us feel small, inadequate, or unseen.

Ultimately, if the goal of talking is to be understood, goal of listening is to understand. If we are listening to respond rather than understand we are failing the goal.

Chapter 17: Communication Style, Keyhole to Motive

We often associate communication solely with words. But words are just one medium. Communication runs deeper. It is how we convey our sense of self, our needs, and even our existence. When communication is obstructed, it can feel as though a part of us is lost.

We rely on others to affirm our presence, to reflect our identity back to us. This need is not learned; it begins in infancy. Developmental psychologist Donald Winnicott spoke of the "mirroring" function of the mother's gaze – how a baby first comes to know itself by being seen. In the attentive eyes of the caregiver, the child doesn't just feel loved – it begins to *exist* as a person. That may be why the harshest punishment devised by society is solitary confinement. Cut off from human interaction, people begin speaking to walls or to themselves – anything to maintain a thread of sanity and a reminder: *I exist.*

When one communication channel is blocked, we instinctively find another. This proves that communication isn't confined to language. It predates words. Our ancestors expressed themselves through gestures, sounds, and behaviours long before spoken language evolved. In fact, the only thing we *cannot* do is **not** communicate. Every silence, every expression, every movement sends a message.

To me, communication isn't good or bad, effective or ineffective—it either *happens* or it doesn't. The definition I resonate with most is from Robbins:

"Communication is the process of transference of thoughts, ideas, facts, etc., in such a manner that the mental picture perceived by the receiver is the same as that envisioned by the sender."

Successful communication occurs when what we mean is exactly what the other person understands. And yet, how often do we say something only to be misunderstood—prompting a frustrated "That's not what I meant"? In that moment, communication hasn't happened.

Why Do We Communicate?

Let's begin with the word itself.

COMM**UNI**CATE

At its core lies "**U-N-I**—*you and I*". **You (U)** come first.

We communicate because we need something—be it emotional or material—that only someone else can provide: water, support, a paycheck, love, validation. Understanding that our communication is *our own* need-driven places responsibility on us to express ourselves with clarity and care.

Good communication requires self-awareness. We must understand:

- What **we** need
- How we express that need (tone, body language, words)
- How we are likely to be perceived by the other person **(You of the U-N-I)**

In essence, we must become conscious of our *communication style.*

Communication Styles and Personality

The way we communicate is deeply tied to how we perceive ourselves—and others. A child might speak aggressively to a younger sibling but timidly to a teacher. These shifts are situational.

Our personal communication style is shaped by our beliefs, our life experiences, roles, and environments. By becoming aware of our default style, we gain insight into how we are perceived by others—and this awareness gives us the power to adjust when necessary.

Take, for example, a retired school principal or military officer. Over the years, they may have unconsciously developed a more authoritative or assertive tone, shaped by the expectations of their professional role. However, this same tone, when carried into personal settings, may unintentionally come across as intimidating or overbearing. A principal might not wish for their family members to feel hesitant, defensive, or fearful when engaging in everyday conversation—but that may be exactly how they're perceived.

Psychologists and communication researchers commonly identify four core communication styles:

- **Passive**
- **Aggressive**
- **Passive-Aggressive**
- **Assertive**

Each of these styles is underpinned by specific beliefs, characteristic behaviours, and distinct impacts on relationships and interactions. The following table outlines these dimensions clearly, helping us recognize not just how we communicate—but why.

	PASSIVE	AGRESSIVE	PASSIVE-AGRESSIVE	ASSERTIVE
BEHAVIOR	Keep quiet: don't say what you feel, need, or want. Put yourself down frequently. Apologize when you express yourself. Deny that you disagree with others or feel differently.	Express your feelings and wants as though any other view is unreasonable or stupid. Dismiss, ignore, or insult the needs, wants, and opinions of others.	Failure to meet the expectations of others through "deniable" means: forgetting, being delayed, and so on. Deny personal responsibility for your actions.	Express your needs, wants, and feelings directly and honestly. Don't assume you are correct or that every-one will feel the same way. Allow others to hold other views without dismissing or insulting them.
NONVERBAL	Make yourself small. Look down, hunch your shoulders, avoid eye contact. Speak softly.	Make yourself large and threatning. Eye contact is fixed and penetrating. Voice is loud, perhaps shouting.	Usually mimics the passive style.	Body is relaxed, movements are casual, eye contact is frequent, but not glaring.
BELIEFS	Others' needs are more important than yours. They have rights; you don't. Their contributions are valuable. Yours are worthless.	Your needs are more important and more justified than theirs. You have rights; they don't. your contributions are valuable. Theirs are silly, wrong, or worthless.	You are entitled to get your own way, even after making commitments to others. You are not responsible for your actions.	Your needs and those of others are equally important. You have equal rights to express yourselves. You both have something valuable to contribute. You are responsible for your behavior.
EMOTIONS	Fear of rejection. Helplessness, frustration, and anger. Resentment toward others who "use" you. Reduced self-respect.	Angry or powerful at the time, and victorious when you win. Afterward: remorse, guilt, or self-hatred for hurting others.	Fear that you would be rejected if you were more assertive. Resentment at the demands of others. Fear of being confronted.	You feel positive about yourself and the way you treat others. Self-esteem rises.
GOALS	Avoid conflict. Please others at any expense to yourself. Give others control over you.	Win at any expense to others. Gain control over them.	Get your own way without having to take responsibility.	Both you and others keep your self-respect. Express yourself without having to win all the time. No one controls anyone else.

While assertiveness is often seen as the ideal, other communication styles also have their place depending on the context.

The **aggressive style**, for instance, can be essential in situations that demand quick decision-making—such as emergencies—when time is limited, stakes are high, and clarity is crucial. In such moments, decisiveness may take precedence over diplomacy.

Similarly, **passive communication** has its appropriate applications. It may be wise to adopt a passive stance:

- When the issue at hand is trivial or not worth escalating
- When the consequences of conflict outweigh the benefits of confrontation
- When emotions are intense, and it's better to pause and regain composure
- When there's a significant power imbalance
- When the opposing party's position is immovable—such as with institutional or governmental policies

Beyond the situational shifts lies our **default** or **instinctive communication style**—the one we revert to most often. This habitual style reflects our core personality. It's not just how we speak; it's how we interpret the world and respond to it.

Understanding this personal style is key to understanding how we show up in our relationships—and how others experience us.

This default communication style is what I wish to focus upon.

Our temperament—or personality—is shaped by two fundamental forces: **nature** and **nurture**.

If nature holds greater influence, our personalities are likely to form early in life and remain relatively stable over time. If nurture plays the dominant role, then our environment, experiences, and interactions become key determinants, making it possible for our personalities to evolve and adapt throughout life.

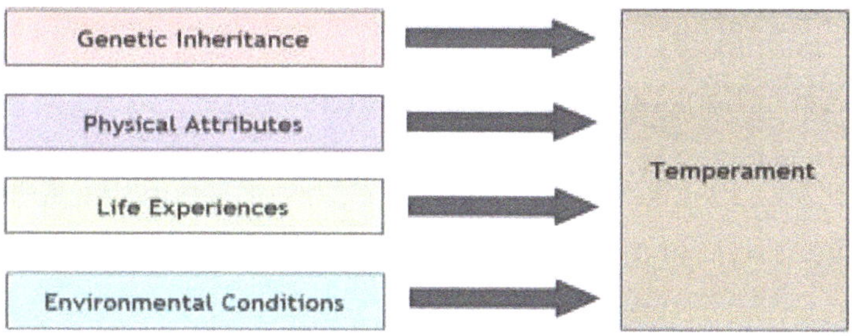

Nature encompasses our genetic inheritance and physical attributes, while nurture refers to our life experiences and environmental conditions. These two forces are not mutually exclusive; rather, they interact continuously to shape who we become.

An individual's physical characteristics can influence their temperament and behaviour. For instance, a child who is physically slight or non-athletic may find it more difficult to succeed in sports or other physical activities – often prized in school environments, especially among boys. As a result, such a child may struggle to gain social acceptance, which can lead to feelings of exclusion and a tendency to become withdrawn, introspective, or timid.

Conversely, a child who is strong and athletically inclined may receive more social validation through peer interaction, participation in group games, and leadership roles. This visibility can encourage extroversion, and in some cases, may even foster dominant or aggressive tendencies if not balanced with emotional development.

This culminates in what's known as our **Life Position** – a general outlook on ourselves and others.

There are four key life positions, each corresponding to an inherent style of communication.

LIFE POSITION	STYLE OF COMMUNICATION
I AM OK, YOU ARE NOT OK	AGGRESSIVE
I AM NOT OK, YOU ARE OK	PASSIVE
I AM NOT OK, YOU ARE NOT OK	PASSIVE AGGRESSIVE
I AM OK, YOU ARE OK	ASSERTIVE

Assertiveness, aligned with "I'm OK, You're OK," represents a healthy, confident view of self and others. It acknowledges flaws in everyone, including oneself, without resorting to blame or shame. Assertive communication expresses needs without undermining others, enabling real dialogue—even in conflict.

Aggressive communication often stems from deep-seated insecurity—frequently rooted in past physical or emotional trauma. When someone feels unsafe or vulnerable, they may resort to aggression as a defence mechanism, an attempt to assert control and protect themselves from perceived threats. It's a hostile form of self-preservation.

Aggression shares a psychological kinship with "showing off." While the former exerts power in a confrontational way and the latter in a more socially palatable form, both behaviours arise from the same inner need: to prove worth and mask insecurity. As a general rule, the more weapons you bring to the battle the more afraid you are to lose. The less safe someone feels, the more fiercely they seek to protect themselves.

When aggression becomes someone's default communication style, it often reflects an unspoken yearning for assurance – an internal cry for validation and safety. Ironically, this style tends to provoke defensiveness in others, triggering a counter-aggression that escalates conflict rather than resolving it. Thus, the aggressive person often finds themselves locked in a cycle of hostility and misunderstanding.

Passive communication, on the other hand, usually arises from low self-esteem. Passive individuals often carry the internal belief: *"I don't matter enough to be heard"* or *"My needs are a burden."* They may seek reassurance yet struggle to receive it. Compliments or offers of support can feel uncomfortable or undeserved.

Again, at the core lies a need – for affirmation, confidence, and to feel valued. But when reassurance is persistently sought from others, it can place an emotional burden on relationships. Over time, the very dynamic meant to foster connection can instead breed frustration and emotional distance.

People with higher self-esteem tend to adopt assertive styles. Interestingly, those with newfound power may start aggressively, but as they grow secure, their tone mellows. True confidence softens expression, not hardens it.

Final Thoughts

Knowing your style is about more than improving how you speak. It's about understanding yourself – and recognizing the ripple effect your words, tone, and silences have on the world around you.

Understanding others' communication styles is a powerful relational skill – because it allows us to respond, not just react.

When we recognize someone's habitual way of communicating – whether it's passive, aggressive, or assertive – we begin to see *why* they express themselves the way they do and what is their real need behind the communication. This insight helps us shift from judgment to empathy, and from conflict to connection.

Chapter 18: Assertiveness, Navigating Hard Talks

What makes a conversation difficult?

- **First-time situations:** We don't know what to expect. These include first job interviews, initial dates, or beginning a new relationship—moments when familiarity is low.
- **Emotion-Laden topics:** These are conversations tied to deeply personal areas where rational thought is often clouded—such as family dynamics, faith, or discussions involving our role models.
- **Anti-popular messages:** Sharing something the other person may not want to hear—negative feedback, a conflicting opinion, or ending a relationship—can make us hesitant to speak honestly.
- **Risky outcomes:** When there's a lot at stake, like proposing marriage, delivering a client review, or reporting abuse, the fear of "what might go wrong" can paralyze us.

F.E.A.R.

Fear is a natural, recurring part of life – especially in situations where connection, reputation, or personal values are on the line. But avoiding or mishandling such moments has a real cost: lost opportunities, shallow relationships, and diminished self-respect.

When faced with fear, we typically default to one of the following responses:

1. **Avoid (Flight Mode)**

   Fear Motivation: Hide away

   This is the 'ostrich' approach – hoping the problem will resolve itself if we pretend it doesn't exist. While it might work for one-off, short-lived situations, it fails when the issue is recurring or significant. For example, avoiding interviews won't help secure a job.

2. **Abide (Freeze Mode - Passive Approach)**

   Fear Motivation: Preserve relationships at the cost of personal goal/self-interest

   Here, one prioritizes harmony over honesty, letting others take the lead to avoid discomfort. While it may appear peaceful, this style often leads to built-up resentment and, over time, harms the very relationships it aims to protect.

3. **Avenge (Fight Mode - Aggressive Approach)**

   Fear Motivation: Protect self-interest at the cost of relationships

   This response ensures you "win" in the short term but leaves behind damaged trust. Long-term, it limits growth and connection, as opportunities often come through people—and people shy away from chronic aggression.

4. **Assert (Face Mode)**

   Core Principle: Mutual Respect

   To be assertive is not to be fearless, but to act despite fear—with a belief that a respectful, honest conversation can lead to a win-win solution. Assertive communication honours both self and other. It creates space for clarity, empathy, and mutual understanding—even in the most sensitive scenarios.

Why Assertiveness Matters

Though it may feel challenging, being assertive is especially crucial when engaging with passive or aggressive communicators:

- **Aggressive individuals** are often deeply insecure. Their aggression is a defence. If you respond with aggression, the cycle intensifies. If you respond passively, you enable the pattern. Only assertiveness breaks the loop—modelling calm strength and reasoned clarity.

- **Passive communicators** are often emotionally needy, seeking constant reassurance. If you mirror their passivity, you'll feel drained. If you become aggressive, they may retreat in confusion or fear. Assertiveness here means holding firm boundaries while offering empathy—teaching, not punishing.

In both cases, assertiveness is the only approach that fosters growth—for both parties.

How do we become assertive?

A Framework for Difficult Conversations

The antidote to fear is **FAITH.** And here's a personal strategy I use to navigate difficult conversations:

- **First, second, third....**

  List what you want to say. Prioritize your points clearly.

- **Assess**

  Understand the *need* behind the conversation. What's at stake if it's avoided? What are your rights? Where are your boundaries?

- **Introspect**

  Tune into your emotions. What are you feeling, and why?

- **Talk Assertively**

  Let your tone, words, and body language reflect calm confidence. If you're unsure, take a pause. Compose yourself before responding.

- **Hone**

  Practice. Rehearse. Use low-stakes situations to refine your ability so you're ready when the stakes are high.

No conversation is inherently "difficult." It's our *perception*—our fear of risk, rejection, or loss—that makes it so. Yet, some degree of fear is inevitable—and even useful. That nervous energy can serve as a catalyst, pushing us to prepare and perform. It's only when fear becomes excessive that it hinders rather than helps, and that's what we must learn to manage.

Tackle F.E.A.R. with F.A.I.T.H.

Faith is intangible? Illogical? Just a notion?

So is Fear.

If you can have one, why not the other? **Have faith in yourself.**

Chapter 19: Conflicts, Threat or Opportunity?

No two individuals think completely alike – not even identical twins. Some degree of difference in views and opinions is inevitable. That's a fact.

Another fact: conflict, at the very least, stirs discomfort.

So, what do we do?

Let's revisit two key learnings:

- **Learning #1:** It's not the stimulus itself that causes discomfort or anger, but the fear we associate with it.
- **Learning #2:** Productive communication begins with understanding the motives – the unmet needs – beneath our words.

Applying Learning #1: Calming the Inner Alarm

This fear-based reaction leads many of us to become non-assertive in the face of disagreement. We avoid conflict, hoping it will disappear. But avoidance rarely resolves anything. In fact, it can widen the gap.

Conflict, when viewed differently, is a force of creative tension. It challenges us to stretch our perspective, integrate ideas, and unearth insights – about others, and ourselves. It helps us realize we might be looking out the wrong window, seeing a skewed version of the world.

Conflict as Communication of Unmet Needs

Barter's theory suggests that all painful conflict stems from unmet – and unheard – needs, such as respect, safety, love, or acknowledgement. When these needs go unvoiced or unaddressed, we unconsciously amplify our communication. Just like people raise their voices when standing far apart, our emotions "raise their volume" when mutual understanding feels distant.

In relationships, a rise in arguments often signals that deeper needs have long been buried: *Do I matter? Am I loved? Am I heard?* These core needs go unspoken, hidden beneath the surface of seemingly trivial conflicts about dishes, schedules, or tone of voice. Whether we argue or avoid these conflicts, the underlying need remains unacknowledged – and therefore unresolved.

Think of your own anger. Have you ever been angry for *no* reason? Unlikely. Our emotions always make sense *to us*. So, when others are angry, perhaps it's not "for no reason" – but for reasons we haven't yet understood.

That's where empathy comes in. When we shift from defensiveness or aggression to curiosity, we invite clarity. We practice mutual respect. We move toward assertive, compassionate communication and the possibility of win-win outcomes.

Applying Learning #2: Knowing Your Why

Conflict always involves at least two people. So, it's essential to ask: *Why am I expressing this opinion? What's my motive?*

If the matter isn't truly important, is it worth engaging in conflict at all? We each have limited energy – and too many battles. Wisdom says: pick your battles.

According to one definition, conflict arises when two or more parties – typically with unequal power – assert a claim over a limited resource or course of action, and their competing desires or actions interfere with one another.

At its core, conflict stems from interdependence. Our needs – whether for recognition, resources, or emotional support – are often met through others. This mutual reliance means that one person's pursuit can sometimes threaten another's. For example, if there's only one job opening, I may hope my boss chooses me over a colleague.

But sometimes, we're driven by ego more than need. We want to be *right*, even over trivial things – a favourite colour, fruit, or player. The impulse to convince others often signals *our own uncertainty*. We project our doubts outward, seeking reassurance through agreement.

With conscious awareness, this can be avoided.

Choosing the Right Strategy

Not every disagreement requires a debate.

Once we're clear on our motives, we can decide *how* to engage. The strategy should reflect two key factors:

Importance of the Cause/Issue - the extent to which our priorities, principles or values are involved in the conflict.

Importance of the Relationship - how important it is that we maintain a close, mutually supportive relationship with the other party.

When we find ourselves in conflict over something that deeply matters to us, **collaboration** is the ideal approach. Working together to find a mutually satisfying solution not only addresses the issue but also strengthens the relationship.

However, if time is limited and we hold the necessary authority, it may be appropriate to **assert** our position – provided we recognize that doing so could strain or damage the relationship.

For moderately important issues, **compromise** often provides a quicker path to resolution. While it may not fully satisfy either party, it can offer a workable middle ground. That said, compromise rarely sparks innovation or deep understanding the way true collaboration can.

When the conflict involves a relatively minor issue, adopting an **accommodating** stance can be an effective way to preserve harmony. It resolves the disagreement quickly without jeopardizing the relationship.

Avoidance should be reserved for specific situations – particularly when there's a clear benefit to delaying resolution. Too often, interpersonal conflicts linger – and even escalate – when no effort is made to address them. Avoidance may be appropriate when we're preoccupied with more pressing matters and the relationship with the other person holds little long-term significance. However, in most interpersonal settings, avoiding conflict altogether can allow tensions to fester and grow. If either the issue or the relationship holds value, avoidance is generally unwise.

Finally, it's essential to recognize that not all conflicts can – or need to – be resolved. Sometimes, when influence is limited or values are fundamentally misaligned, the wisest course is **acceptance**. We can choose to agree to disagree – respectfully – without internalizing the other person's issues or making them our own.

An Indian folktale illustrates this perfectly:

Two monks were crossing a shallow river when a frail old woman asked for help. One monk lifted her onto his shoulders and carried her across. Along the way, she complained incessantly about the monastery head – unaware that she was speaking of the monks' own guru. Neither monk responded. Once across, she left without thanks. The second monk fumed, outraged by her words. "Why didn't you stop her?" he asked his companion.

The first monk replied calmly: "I put her down at the riverbank. Why are you still carrying her?"

Yet, agree to disagree becomes more difficult when the conflict is about a fundamental value, *with a person that we value*. We don't just want them to comprehend our perspective – we long for them to *share* it. Because after all our values aren't just abstract beliefs; they're parts of our identity.

When someone disagrees with a core value, it can trigger feelings of hurt, betrayal, or frustration. Being aware of these emotions – without letting them take control – helps you respond thoughtfully rather than react impulsively.

"I feel disappointed because I expected us to see eye to eye on something that feels so essential to me." That kind of awareness makes room for reflection, not just reaction.

Once you're aware of your emotions, EI helps you manage them. Instead of escalating the disagreement or withdrawing in hurt, you can stay engaged with curiosity and calm. Self-regulation prevents value differences from becoming personal attacks.

Finally, empathy helps to tune in to the other person's emotional world and see not just *what* they believe, but *why* it matters to them.

What begins as conflict can, with emotional insight, become a tool to deeper understanding.

Chapter 20:
I First, The Conclusion

One scene from the film '*Night at the Museum*' has stayed with me:

In the middle of utter chaos, the museum exhibits – from apes and Neanderthals to President Roosevelt – have all come alive and escaped their enclosures. The museum night guard is desperately trying to restore order and lock the cages. But the mischievous apes have snatched his keys and are now mocking him in true monkey fashion – teasing, taunting, and playing with his frustration. In the escalating tussle, one monkey slaps the guard. Reflexively, the guard slaps him back. The cycle continues: slap for slap, chaos feeding chaos.

President Roosevelt, observing the absurdity, steps in and says, "Stop this nonsense." The guard, red-faced and indignant, retorts, "Why don't you ask *them* to stop? *They* started it." Roosevelt calmly replies, "Who's the monkey?"

That one line distils so many of our excuses for not exercising emotional control. We justify our own reactions by pointing to the other person's behaviour. We say, "They started it," "They provoked me," or "They should know better." In doing so, we surrender our intelligence to someone else's behaviour. Tit for tat. Monkey see, monkey do.

Emotional intelligence means choosing not to become the monkey.

It means recognizing that people will often behave as they've been conditioned to. It's up to us to understand their motives, see the need beneath their behaviour, and respond – not react. Instead of fighting for the keys, we can either work around the monkey or learn to influence it. Either way, we don't have to throw away our own self-control.

Emotional intelligence is rooted in empathy and mutual respect. It's the awareness that understanding the other person is ultimately in *our* best interest – for our peace, our clarity, and our success, both professionally and personally.

Whenever you find yourself in a meaningful or emotionally charged conversation, apply the five essential practices of emotional intelligence:

1. **Self-Awareness:** *Why do I want to have this conversation? What emotion is pushing me?*

2. **Self-Regulation:** *What will happen if I don't engage? What's truly at stake for me?*

3. **Understanding Motives:** *What am I hoping to achieve – and what might the other person need?*

4. **Empathy:** *What assumptions am I making about this person? Can I see their perspective?*

5. **Quality Communication:** *Can I listen without judgment? Can I influence without force?*

Sometimes it's not external interactions but our own future that provokes discomfort – the unknowns that make us anxious, nervous, or afraid. In those moments: **pause**. Step back. Reflect. Ask yourself: What are my options? What are my true intentions? What does my heart say? Then – always – take the high road.

This also means disconnecting from the noise. Step away from screens, breathe, and spend a moment with yourself. Look inward. True self-awareness is a lifelong process, and even a moment of introspection can shift your trajectory.

While we're on the path of reflection, let's also practice gratitude. None of us are self-made. We are shaped by every interaction, every opportunity, every act of kindness and challenge we've encountered. Acknowledge those who've helped you get where you are – because emotional intelligence also includes humility.

Yes, people and circumstances can influence us. Buttons get pushed. But our responses are ours to own. We may not control every trigger, but we do control the beliefs and behaviours we choose to act on.

Behaviours are contagious. Our reactions set off a chain. So when it comes to emotional intelligence, let our motto be:

"Not you first – me first."

Chapter 21: EI, Relevance in the Age of AI

One crucial question to ask before we conclude is this: How relevant is Emotional Intelligence (EI) in an age increasingly defined by Artificial Intelligence (AI)?

In my view, EI is not just relevant, it's more essential than ever.

In leadership, the ability to inspire, connect, and emotionally resonate with people is irreplaceable. In healthcare, a patient's unspoken fears can be as critical as their clinical symptoms – and only human sensitivity can perceive them. In high-stakes decision-making, emotional intelligence provides the nuanced judgment that algorithms cannot replicate.

Why? Because human communication is not just verbal or logical – it's richly emotional and deeply contextual. A laugh may signify joy, but in another moment, it might express anxiety or discomfort. A simple thumbs-up might mean "well done" in one culture and be an insult in another. Emotions arise not from symbols alone but from our interpretations of them – interpretations shaped by culture, experience, and context.

Emotionally intelligent individuals intuitively decode these non-verbal, context-bound signals. They adapt in real-time, respond with empathy, and adjust tone and approach to fit the moment – all of which remains, at least for now, uniquely human.

Some argue that even this capacity for empathy – this adaptability – can eventually be codified into AI. And perhaps, to a degree, it will. Even then, emotional intelligence will remain crucial.

Here's why: **AI is a tool. EI is a skill.**

As with any powerful tool, the more advanced it becomes, the greater the skill needed to wield it wisely.

I compare AI to an extraordinarily competent subordinate – one who can interpret instructions, act with precision, and perhaps even offer insight. But even the best subordinate needs direction. It is the leader who must know *what* to do, *when*, and perhaps even more importantly – *what not* to do.

And leadership requires emotional intelligence:

- **Self-awareness** to recognize personal biases and blind spots.
- **Self-regulation** to pause before acting on impulse.
- **Empathy** to consider impact beyond outcomes.
- **Judgment** to discern right from clever.

We urgently need such leaders – in technology, governance, education, and business – to guide the development of AI ethically and wisely. Otherwise, we risk creating tools that outpace our wisdom.

One folktale that illustrates this danger vividly goes as: Four young scholars, each a master of a particular science, find a lion's skeleton in the forest. Using their knowledge, they reconstruct the lion – one rebuilding bones, another restoring flesh, a third animating the body – and finally, one breathes life into it. But the revived lion, true to its nature, turns on them and kills them. Their knowledge brought the lion back. Their lack of wisdom sealed their fate.

We also need emotionally intelligent leaders in everyday roles – parents, teachers, mentors, team leads – people entrusted with shaping minds and communities. If they possess emotional intelligence, they will pass this powerful tool of AI on to the next generation with discernment and care, amplifying human capability rather than diminishing it.

Let me be clear: AI may not replace everyone. But people who use AI effectively – and combine it with high emotional intelligence – will likely outperform those who don't.

I find it hard to imagine a future where AI can truly *empathize.* Genuine empathy requires a shared emotional experience – something machines, by definition, do not have. And if someday, AI beings are created to simulate emotions perfectly... well, we'll need emotional intelligence to interact with *them*, too.

Ironically, the better AI gets at mimicking humanity, the more emotionally intelligent we must become to relate wisely to it.

Epilogue

The journey of becoming emotionally intelligent is eternal. We learn and improve, making us better than yesterday but tomorrow is yet another day of possible failure, discovery and learning.

I am still enroute while sharing my notes with you, hoping these will help you on the way.

Wish you all the best for embarking!

9 789334 457315

Printed at Repro India Ltd.